Soulful Expressions

※※※※※
Inspirational Poetry
※※※※※

by

Sy'needa Penland

Copyright © 2019 by Sy'needa Penland

All rights reserved. No part of this book may be reproduced or trans-mitted in any form or by any means electronic or mechanical, including photocopy, recording or any information storage and retrieval system now known or to be invented, without permission in writing from the author and publisher. The exception would be in the case of brief quotations embodied in the critical articles or reviews and pages where permission is specifically granted by the author and publisher. Any members of educational institutions wishing to photocopy part or all of the work for classroom use, or publishers who would like to obtain permission to include in an anthology, should send inquiries to:

Adeenys Publishing
P. O. Box 716
Dacula, GA 30019
adeenyspublishing@gmail.com

Printed in the United States

Book design by Sy'needa Penland

ISBN-13: 978-1-942863-05-2

FIRST EDITION

This book is dedicated to the Soulful Expressions of the Heart.

Contents

A Leader of Vision	*10*
Acceptance	*11*
Age of Enlightenment	*12*
All-Seeing Soul	*13*
Angelic Life	*15*
As My Spirit is Set Free	*16*
Awaken Yourself	*17*
Beautiful, Earthly Star	*18*
Beloved Mother Earth	*19*
Birth of Humanity	*20*
Black Seed, Unchanged	*21*
Bold and Beautiful	*23*
Born With It	*24*
Call Me *GOD*	*25*
Cardinal Laws of Balance	*26*
Celebration of Peace and Love	*27*
Center of thy Universe	*28*
Choices	*29*
Come Judgement Day	*30*
Compound, My Earth	*31*

Confidence	*33*
Conformity	*34*
Cosmic Forces	*35*
Cradled Essence of Life	*36.*
Creative Genius	*37*
Creed of Love	*38*
Crimes Against Humanity	*39*
Cross Roads	*40*
Dark Shadows	*41*
Darkness	*42*
Deliverance	*43*
Divine Chord of Life	*44*
Divine Love	*45*
Divine Radiance	*46*
Divine Spirit	*47*
Divine Universe	*49*
Divine Worth	*50*
Earth, is All Life	*52*
Electromagnetic Energy	*53*
Embodiment of Life	*54*
Energy	*55*
Eternal Flame	*56*
Everlasting Love	*57*
Expressions, Purity of Love	*58*
Final Thoughts	*61*
Flawless	*62*
Floetry	*63*
Forever in Love	*64*

Free	*65*
Free Spirited Energy	*66*
Galactic Essence	*68*
Give Me Strength	*69*
Goddess of Divine Love	*70*
Ground Thy Soul to Thee	*71*
Harmony	*72*
Hate and Strife	*73*
Hate, Rest in Peace	*74*
Heart of the Divine	*75*
Hello to Love	*76*
Higher Good	*77*
History is No Longer His to Tell	*78*
How to Mend a Broken Heart	*79*
Human Evolution	*80*
Human Race	*81*
I AM, Life	*82*
I AM, the Universe	*83*
I Bestow, Love	*84*
Indigenous is My Soul	*85*
I Set You Free	*87*
I Surrender My Free Will	*88*
If I Do More, I Go Farther	*89*
In Jesus' Name	*90*
Infinite Universe	*92*
Injustice to Mother Earth	*94*
Invitation to Life	*95*
Justice For All	*96*

Karma	*97*
Lady Evening Star	*98*
Lava	*99*
Laws of Nature	*100*
Life's Challenges	*101*
Like Dust, You Rise	*102*
Love Orbits Evolution	*104*
Loving Blessings	*105*
Luna Moon	*106*
Make Love, Not War	*107*
Milky Way	*108*
Misunderstood	*109*
Moral Duty	*110*
Morning Delight	*111*
My Spirit Yells	*112*
Natural Beauty	*113*
Natural Essence of the Universe	*114*
Natural Hair	*115*
Not Upon My Flesh	*116*
Pain Shall Exist No More	*117*
Peace, in the Wake of Evil	*118*
Peaceful is My Earth	*119*
Play	*120*
Power of Desire	*121*
Praise	*122*
Protector of My Soul	*124*
Queendom of Love	*125*
Raw Emotions	*126*

Rebirth of Divinity	*127*
Receive Me in Kind	*128*
Relax	*129*
Rest in Peace	*130*
Resurrection Day	*131*
Sacred Waters	*132*
Salvage thy Earth	*133*
Save My Soul	*134*
Self-Destruction	*135*
She Sustains Me	*136*
Silver Lining of Hope	*137*
Sins Against Humanity	*138*
Soul Healing	*139*
Soul Mate	*140*
Soul of Compassion	*141*
Soul Wealth	*142*
Sound of the Universe	*143*
Sovereign Queendom	*144*
Spirit of Hate	*145*
Spirits Take Flight	*146*
Spirits of the Underworld	*147*
Spoken Word Poetry	*148*
Surrender	*149*
Survival of the Fittest	*150*
Sweet, is the Fragrance of Love	*151*
Temper Thy Soul	*152*
The Abundance of Love	*153*
The Almighty Sun	*155*

The Art of My Essence	*156*
The Gift of Life is Love	*157*
The Menagerie of Life	*161*
The Perfect Union	*162*
The Universe Shall Speak	*163*
The Veil of Hell	*164*
Thrive	*165*
Today's a New Day	*146*
Twin Flame	*167*
Umbilical Cord of Life	*168*
Unfoldment of Divine Love	*169*
Universal Essence	*170*
Universal Guidance	*171*
Universal Stars	*172*
Vow	*173*
We Shall Evolve in Love	*174*
We Shall Rise	*175*
When I Hear Music	*176*
White Beauty	*177*
Why Does My Genius Offend You	*178*
X-Rated Soul	*179*
You Are The Power	*180*
Zeal	*181*

Soulful Expressions

A Leader of Vision

President Donald Trump,
As you sit atop America's throne,
Let not your *Empire*, fall like *Rome*!
As you build your *Wall*, to defend *our ports?*
Do not allow your judgment
To be of that of distort—
By the craft of *negative sorcery* of sorts.

As **great men** have stood long before you,
Allow their legacies to guide all that you do.
As justice seek to prevail,
And *victory* you seek to claim,
Hear first the cry of the people,
To avoid a legacy of shame!!

Acceptance

When will the energy of hate
manifest into acts of kindness
towards a person of a different kind?
Why has the nakedness of the human soul
blinded thine eyes to see the loving spirit
of that of another?

As fathers and mothers conceive
the most precious gift known to man,
The art of reproduction—
For modern-day evolution
has led the loving soul astray,
towards the likeness of the wicked;

Such energy has become fuel
for the imaginary minds, who seek
to conceive the energy of chaos,
as their egos attempts to prove
or disprove, one theory, or another—

When implanted beliefs are challenged
by the laws of human behavior, not nature,
the *enlightened* mind then seeks to controls
the collective *Spirits* that exists
within all realms of human existence,
as *Universal wisdom* passes down
from one generation to another.

Time— Space— Void— Matter,
or whatever name or "inventions"
that's been brought about by humankind,
is not named or measured in the *Galactic Universe,*
it simply just is… *Acceptance!*

Age of Enlightenment

Fluidity of the mind
Intertwines with all that is,
All that once was— Reality.
As history is being repeated
Before our eyes.

In modern-day society,
Artificial has become implanted in the
Intelligent mind—
As if it once was *(artificial)*.

As the *Age of Enlightenment* is upon us,
Key minds will rise above—
Humanity must be saved
By the collective masses,
As the *designers* of our daily lives
Attempt to reorganize the classes;

Hold on to what you will have left
Which is the *Soul of the Universe*—
For if you *believe* in *Divine Will,*
It will break any curse!

All-Seeing Soul

Polarities of the heart
Shall not tear us apart,
We've been down this road before,
Centuries ago,
When we last settled old scores.

As our young, continues to die young,
Who can we count on
To fight our ongoing battles…
"Artificial Intelligence?"

Yet, here lies the problem,
Artificial realities of the human mind,
That remains blind
To matters of the heart.

As the *Soul of the Universe,*
Brings collective life back together again,
We shall live as *One Being,*
Under the *Great Spirit*
Of the *all-seeing soul* of thy *Mother Earth.*
For her body, encapsulates all life form
Within her *Divine Essence*—

As generations, come and go;
As she recedes with her tides;
As her mountainous empires rise
And falls, to become flatlands
For man-made battlefields;
As her *airspace* absorbs all that mankind
Has left to offer;
As the human race continues to be defiant
To our *Divine Creator*— We shall awaken
The *Spirit of Father Time.*

For *Father Time*, is the timekeeper
Of the *Universe's* soul,

As he awakens her to end the race
That will no longer be part of
Her loving tapestry,
As she prepares her fertile *Earth*
To rebirth loving and compassionate beings,
To become ambassadors of *LOVE*.

Let us not look above for salvation,
Let's look within, to repent for the sins
Of the past, present, and future,
As our super-human strength
Is put to the ultimate test, to soothe
The soul of the *Universe* to rest.

Let us strengthened our hearts
With *love* and *compassion,*
To become an everlasting
Species, to thrive upon thy Earth.
In our collective being, we shall trust,
Not to repeat the *will* of the past,
Or self-destruct, but fulfill our destiny,
To preserve humanity!
Once more!

Angelic Life

I Am, many things,
And many things
Are of me—
I Am, all things,
And all things
Are of me;

I Am, the sacred core
Of the human soul,
Through my *Divine Spirit*
All life unfolds—
Through one's life journey
My tales are told;

Rebirthed seeds
Upon thy sacred *Earth,*
As I give rebirth
To *Angelic life—*
Broken are the curses
That harbors strife;

As *Peace* and *Love*
Conjoin all souls
To become one,
Under the *Divine* light
Of the *Sun—*
My *Crescent Moon*
Shall forever nourish
The souls of thee;

As I my Divine *essence*
Take root in thy holy ground,
Forever compound
Shall be thy Earth,
As she rebirths all life,
In the kindred Spirit
Of the *Divine Universe.*

As My Spirit is Set Free

What is happening to me.
Screams my soul,
What is happening to me,
As my Spirit is set Free.
I'm finally Free!
Free to be me.
I'm free to be at peace
With Love and Harmony
I'm free.

Awaken Yourself

Awaken your *mind,*
 to *Spirit.*

Awaken your *soul,*
 to *Flesh.*

Awaken your *flesh,*
 to *Love.*

Awaken yourself,
 to *Being.*

Beautiful, Earthly Star

Compassion,
Is my vow to you,
As I stand beneath
Your night sky;

You sing to me,
Sweet lullabies
Of your beautiful essence,
Quintessence
Of your vast *Universe;*

With each poetic verse,
I feel the love you bestow
To your *Divine, Earthly Creations*;

What a soul-felt sensation
You inspire in me, from afar,
The embodiment of *love*
For your *Beautiful, Earthly Star.*

Beloved Mother Earth

Behold, *Truth,*
Speak through
To my soul,
As *Divine Life*
Of *Mother Universe*
Unfolds…

Ground thy *Spirit*
In thy creative essence,
The mystical-magical
Quintessence of you.

Forever guide my being
As you ground thy presence
To the beloved soul of you,
Mother Earth!

Birth of Humanity

To understand the mind of GOD
Is to feel the heart
Of the *Divine Universe*
When she rebirths
All of her *Divine Creations*—

Her cosmic sensations
Are felt throughout
Her galaxies,
As she rebirths her soul
Again and again,
To *infinity*.

Simply lie still
And open your heart
As her synergy
Ignites a divine spark
Of love and compassion
Through the relaxation
Your mind—

As she entwines herself
With the soul of the *Earth*,
As she did when she
First gave birth to humanity.

Black Seed, Unchanged

Unchanged, is my *Earth*.
Unchanged, is my *Mind*.
Unchanged, is my *Vernacular*.
Unchanged, is my *DNA*.

Born as a *black man*,
From the seed of the *I AM*,
Not a replica of
Science experimentation,
Seeking to prove a *theory of creation*.

To study my birth,
Is to explore the essence
Of thy *Universe*—
Beyond the boundaries
Of the controlled mind.
Beyond the mundane cycles
Of your everyday life.

Caged boxes— Incubators.
Fabricated homes
Where familiar *Spirits* roam.
Luxury cars entraps my soul,
As I travel along
The roller coaster of life.

Each encounter with another life form
Awakens my curiosity,
And excites possibilities of
Creating a *New Me*—
Mirrored reflections of the ego,
Now stands before another being.

To be judged for my deeds.
To be judged for my behavior.
To be judged for my words.
To be judged for my actions.
To be judged for my skin color.

To be judged for my gender.
To be judged for my choices,
On how I chose to live my life.

I am labeled,
I am stereotyped—
To become a prototype
For designer goods and services.
To become a human mannequin,
A fleshly coated *robot*—
Something artificial
In another man's eyes.
Non-human.

Money, power, greed,
And the obsession to control
Another being will eventually strip
Humanity of the beauty
And natural essence of *Divine* life,
To be replaced with replicas
Of artificial beings—
For I am immune to such creations,
Because *I Am* melanin.
A *black seed*— *Unchanged.*

Bold and Beautiful

Bold and Beautiful,
I shall ordain you—
Fearless,
Is what you shall be.
As you give birth,
To preserve humanity

Within thy core,
I shall plant thou seed.
Upon rebirth,
I shall provide for all needs.

Caretakers of thy beloved Earth,
I shall entrust upon you!

Upon thou return,
I shall reward you
With truth of who you are.
For now, I shall call you,
My Divine, Earthly Stars.

Born With It

Why do I need to defend
That which defends itself,
It's Divine-Self
It's Infinite-Self
It's Radiant-Self
Its's Beautiful-Self
It's Selfless-Self
It's Compassionate-Self
It's Original-Self
It's Universal-Self
It's Galactic-Self
It's Powerful-Self
It's Dominant-Self
It's Whole-Self
It's Graceful-Self
It's Loving-Self

Melanin...
You have to be born with it,
To understand!

Call Me GOD

For I carry the force of nature
Beneath my wings,
Day or night
My *Spirit* transforms
Into many things
Call me *GOD*,
It doesn't matter
Because my Vibration
Shatters
All forms
To conform
To the *Spirit of Love*.

Cardinal Laws of Balance

Only in America,
Will you find a heart— *Blind*
To respect the *Flesh* of another kind,
To respect the *Spirit* of another kind
To respect the *Morals* of another kind,
To respect the *Cardinal ways*
Of an anguished heart,
That will never part
The *Cardinal ways* of the *Divine Will*—

As my devout quill
Speaks to the hollow souls of mankind,
Let us not be blind to *justice*.
For open thine eyes to see
The *Cardinal Laws of Balance*
That *Lady Justice* shall bring.

Let us sing, in unison, to deliver
The anguished soul
To its final resting place,
To bring about equality
On matters of *Gender, Race*
And *Free Will*.

For the *will* of thou flesh
Shall thrive to do its best,
In its conquest for success
But shall not prey upon
The flesh of another kind!

Celebration of Peace and Love

As we welcome in the *Season of Love*,
Those of us that are in harmony
With the *Divine Universe,*
Shall conduct our daily rituals
To celebrate *Peace* and *Love.*
Therefore, I ask our *leaders* to put
Their *hate* and *differences* aside,
And respect our time of worship
And prayer!!

Center of thy Universe

Welcome to my inner yoke,
With each word spoke*(en)*
From your core,
Curses broken,
As *Spirits* soar—

I shall guide you
To the center of thy *Universe,*
With each poetic verse.

As the spoken-word
Ignites living creations,
Feel my loving vibrations
Within your heart—

Created from but a single spark
Of *Divine Love,*
As below— In-between,
So above.

We shall become
What we create,
As loving thoughts
Conquers all—
Including, hate.

Choices

Life is filled with choices.
To surrender thy will to change
Is oftentimes a choice unwelcomed.

Complacency,
Is a conditioned mindset,
Unaccepting of change.

Freedom of the Spirit,
Is a choice to be
Open-minded and *full of life*

Matters of the heart
Is a choice, to liken
And experience the *joys of love.*

Come Judgement Day

One day soon,
We must all meet our *Divine Creator*
To raise our hands to thee,
To swear to the energy
That manifested the fate
That led to the self-destruction
Of humanity—
The overwhelming energy of hate.

Upon our reincarnation,
We must take a vow to surrender
To the ultimate defender,
The *Energy of Divine Love,*
That *Earth's Universe* creates,
Within our hearts and souls,
As *Divine Life* unfolds
To calibrate our thoughts from within;
Before committing a cardinal sin,
We must pledge an oath to thee,
The essence of our origin;

As the *Great Divine* entwines
Her essence with our
Spirits, bodies and minds,
We shall preserve the fate
Of *All* life forms, that she creates,
And manifest the energy of *Love,*
To conquer the origin of *Hate.*

Compound, My Earth

When my mind feels discombobulated,
My energy becomes coagulated,
My *Spirit* becomes regulated,
My body feels weighted
From all the chaos that distorts
My free flowing energy.

Oceans swells inside me,
As blood rushes to my surface—
Like lava pouring from the cavity of my soul.
Layers of new life rejuvenates inside me,
As Divine essence, nourishes
That which flourishes deep within my flesh.

As *Air's* gentle breeze cools my soul,
With each breath—
Passion rises beneath my skin.
New life begins, again.

Compound, my *Earth*.
Solid—
The ground beneath my feet.
Oceans, rises to the heights of my *cosmic galaxy*.
Celestial heights of my *Divine Universe*.
As *She,* becomes *Me*.

Wisdom and understanding pours into my soul.
Her mold— Shattered. Like broken glass.
Crystalline fragments of *her* soul—
Cosmic pathway to her inner worlds,
Beyond human comprehension.

> *Diamonds*
> *Rubies*
> *Sapphires*
> *Amethyst*
> *Quartz crystals, and more…*

Essential elements of her *Earth*.
Fragments of her inner soul,
Surface to realms above—
Darkness' veil, unveiled,
As the *Divine Universe* dances
In a ritual of love.

Confidence

The inability to see your own faults,
And accept personal blame,
Creates a desire to prove
That you are always right,
Perfect— Flawless,
Causes you to improve yourself,
Perfect yourself;
Thus allowing you to become
More ambitious to achieve
Anything.

Hence, instead of becoming
Caught-up in self-pity,
And dwelling over
What others think of you,
You will eventually
Become more positive,
Which makes you
A better person,
And more successful.

Conformity

Conformity, has become the new *Normality,*
And *artificial mediums,* attempts to control
Our *original thoughts.*

Yet the stimulation of artificial sensations
Becomes opportunities for *Divine* manifestation
Of the soul, to unfold *new seeds of life*—
The *Spirit of Love* evolves humanity
When faced with extreme *strife.*

When *Free Will,* is challenged,
The *Universe* relieves the tension
On the mind, as well as the confines
Of *Conformity.*

Cosmic Forces

Cosmic forces, I bestow,
Loving energy down *below,*
As *above*, I harness love,
In-between, it shall be,
Blessing of *Cosmic* energy.

As I heal your hearts,
We shall never part.
All entities *below* and *above*
Shall be grounded in *love*.

As *Air* is to *Fire,*
I fulfill your desires.
As *Water* is to *Earth,*
All life, rebirthed.

May your heavens within
Be cleansed of sin,
As I restore my *Love*
Upon thy *Earth,*
As *she* is rebirthed—

Love in the air,
Love everywhere,
Love it shall be,
As my *Earthly* souls
Are filled with *cosmic,*
Loving energy.

Cradled Essence of Life

As humanity evolves,
The Cradled Essence of Life
Seeks to host a new *being*.

Cosmic replicas
Of the *Divine*
Entwines her *Spirit*
With the embryonic cord
Of human life.

Each time her essence rebirths,
Curses are lifted—
And a new generation of gifted
Souls, are bestowed upon
Thy *Earthly Queendom*.

To evolve the essence
Of humanity, during its transit
To *Infinity*.

Creative Genius

I invite you
to explore
my canvas,
I call *Earth*.

As I give birth
to my
creative genius
of ecstasy—

Where *love*
is my devotion
to *Divine Energy*—
As she excites
all emotions
of your sensory.

Fell my harmonic
vibrations of touch,
feel and taste—
As I awaken you
to embrace
all of me.

Eyes shut,
open wide.
Explore inside—
My cavity.
My soul center.
My hollow *Earth*.
As I give birth
to you.

Creed of Love

When you live a life of *Higher Purpose*,
You naturally *understand*
That you are in harmony
With the *collective soul*
Of the *Divine Universe*.
Who in times of turmoil and despair,
Reconditions our hearts with *Love*, to repair
The broken souls of humanity.

As we celebrate the *Loving Essence*
Of our *Divine Mother*,
The *Creator* and *Preserver*
Of *All* living beings,
We shall come together in
Peace and Unity
To end the discord of those
Who seek to disrespect
Her *Earthly Queendom*.

May her unconditional *Love*
Be everlasting, as she reinforces
The *Spirit of Compassion*,
As we preserve the *Creed of Love*,
And vow to never stray
From her *Universal* teachings;
To hold humanity accountable
For the actions that brought about
Our self-afflictions,
As well as our addictions,
To *War*, *Love* and *Peace*.

Crimes Against Humanity

Crimes against humanity
   Has led to modern-day insanity—
Mankind seeking to control
   The souls of another.

Oh' how wicked thy mothers
   Have become— Not protecting
Thy righteous sons;
   Turning them over to
Captives of the wild.

Wild kingdoms of the *Earth*—
   Rebirthed ecosystems of life.
Strife amongst the realms of human nature
   Must one-day meet its maker,
To repent for sins committed against thyself.

Cross Roads

I've been tested
All my life,
I've never rested,
I don't like strife.

But here I go,
Down this road
Once again—

My heart is stronger.
Yet here I stand,
Along this journey,
Once again!

The world around me,
Engulfed in sin—
As I thrive,
To survive,
My heart grows strong,
To live on,
Until I meet the crossroads
Once again.

Dark Shadows

Carry my thoughts
Into the wind,
As I sing to you.

Allow my *Universal Spirit*
To guide all that you do.

Shackles broken,
Mind released,
Awaken to reality.

Illusions of life,
Hollow shells,
Spirits' fantasy.

Bodies controlled
By puppet masters,
Who spell the mind,
To see *dark shadows* of life.
To reshape your reality.

Darkness

Darkness rises
From the abyss
Of thy *Earth*
And takes hold
Of thee,
Surrender to its will—
Divine Loving Energy;
When greeted by
The light of day,
A ray of hope
Shall guide the way
To infinite galaxies
Beyond thy Universe.

Deliverance

Before I release,
Compound my *Earth*—
Explosion of rebirth,
As she ignites the passion
Within my soul.

As I unfold, pure ecstasy,
For the entire *Universe* to see,
I must ground myself
In thy natural essence.

Her presence is all around.
Thy *Earth*, compound—
Soul rebirthed;
Divine-Saging of my mind,
As our essence intertwines
As she delivers thy fertile youth,

Love and compassion
Ferments within my heart
As old nature departs—
My body enriched,
As she provides for
All of my needs.

Earth, I return to you,
Delivered.

Divine Chord of Life

The *Divine Chord of Life*
is where I'm strung.
Rhythmic movement,
beats her drum.

Universal vibrations,
synergetic energy—
Mystical pathway
into realms
that the naked eye
cannot see.

Neither touch nor taste
reveals her face,
but feel her *Divine* essence
as she pulsates
every fiber of your being.

Transmutable.
Majestic.
Vibrant.
Divine energy.

Divine Love

Familiar, is my essence.
Familiar, is my form.
Familiar, is my voice
Familiar, is my choice.

Familiar, is my history,
In reshaping the Universe
To its original form,
As it was designed to be.

As below,
So above,
I hereby reshape
All matter in-between,
Into the essence of
Divine Love.

Divine Radiance

Behold,
I unfold,
Divine Radiance.

Infused
from the
sacred chambers
of my soul.

Divine lotus
within thy skin.
Akin to *all*
living beings.

A living replica
of Mother Earth's,
Divine Energy.

Divine Spirit

The *One* who calls
himself my *Savior*,
I invite you to
my *Divine* lair,
which house my
eternal flame;

Extinguish my
sinful desires,
rescue me from the
fallacies of illusions,
that occupies the *matter*
which envelopes
thy *Earth;*

Artificial matter
of the self-reflection
of humanity,
where all *self-will*
is suppressed
by disillusioned thoughts
of your existence;

Reveal yourself
before thine eyes
of humanity.

Be still, thy Earth.
Be still, thy Heart.
Be still, thy Flame.
Be still.

No sound.
No thought..
No pulse.
No matter.
No void.

Only *I*, *Divine Spirit*,
the *air* you breathe.
I give life to your eternal soul—
Reincarnation of *thy-self*.

Divine Universe

O' Divine Mother Earth,
I surrender my soul to thee.
Protect me in this realm,
as you heal humanity.

As you rise, to their demise,
to cleanse the souls of thee—
I shall be an instrument
for the *Divine Universe,* as *she*
incarnate the souls of thee;

Within our hearts, *Spirits* take part,
to proclaim their *Earthly* seeds.
No longer shall our hearts bleed
for the sake of greed—
Yet for the *Universal* power
born into thee;

As *Air* is to *Earth,* we shall rebirth
a generation of righteous men.
No longer will they sin,
in the name of thee;

As *Water* is to *Fire,*
fuel the passion of their
desire, to bring forth *love*
once again.

Divine Worth

The oppressed soul
Knows not the value
Of his *Divine worth*,
As he seeks clearer
Understanding of himself—
His soul purpose to *Mother Earth*.
Upon his pathway to the *Divine*,
He must break through the shackles
that *institutes* his mind.

It was— Is not *He*,
That carries the seeds
Of *Divine* life—
One who provides
The protective womb,
The physical embodiment
of thy *Earth*— Who births
Life into humanity!

It was— Is not *He*,
Whose umbilical cord
Connects the fetus
To the *Divine Universe*,
From *gestation*,
To *transmutation*,
To *reincarnation*,
To *birth*.

It was— Is not *He*,
Who carries the
Divine placenta sac—
The *Sacred Womb of Life*;

It was— Is not *He*,
Who the *Divine Universe*
Chose to birth its delicate seeds,
Like other floral essence
of *Her Divine Earth*.

It is *He*,
The *Divine Universe*
Entrusts to watch over
Her Divine Earth,
And care for
All of *Her* creations,
From *gestation*,
To *transmutation*,
To *reincarnation*,
To re*birth*.

Bestowed upon
Woman and child,
Including those connected
To her Wild— *Queendom;*
To nurture an *evolved*
Generation of *Divine,*
Spiritual beings!

Earth, is All Life

Mother Earth,
You are my *Universe.*
There is no other *planet* like you.

You are my heaven.
You are my *Loving Star.*
I am the mirrored reflection of you.

Your *Spirit* is my *flesh.*
Your *being* is my *soul.*
Your *essence* is my *mind,*
Where all *truth* unfolds.

Our *union* was upon conception,
When you gave birth to me,
To be a blessing in this realm,
To nourish the *souls* of humanity.

Electromagnetic Energy

Evil comes in many forms and fashions,
Passion envelopes the fibers of my soul,
Infused by the electromagnetic energy of love.

I don't stray far away from my heart's center!

Magnetic core of the *Earth,* is where my *Spirit* lies,
In harmony as *one*, our energy magnifies.
As we emit our star dust to the heavenly skies,
Our passion shall purify your soul.

Embodiment of Life

As the heart seeks
To achieve love,
In the embodiment
Of an environment
Filled with hate,
It merely becomes
A manifestation of itself,
When hate has no other place
To go.

Energy

Essence
Nourishes
Each
Ray of
God, in
You

Eternal Flame

Unleashed *Spirits*,
Bearers of the Eternal Flame;
Risen from the swamps of the bayous—
Anguished souls, with no name.

For centuries, I have nourished you,
guiding your pathway to the *eternal flame,*
to be released from purgatory—
Freedom, you shall proclaim.

There is no better vengeance
than to break the cycle of rebirth;
As your *Spirits* provide a gateway
to the *heavens*—
To live as *one,* with the *Universe.*

Chains, broken.
Curses, lifted.
Blessed are the chosen ones,
as you lend a helping hand, to the gifted.

Stars, above,
Stars, below,
Seeds of love—
Upon thy *Earth,* you shall bestow.

Everlasting Love

O' Heavenly Divine,
I rightfully decline,
submitting my essence to
the *chaotic forces*
of negative energy.

Praise to the *Most High,*
as darkness passes us by,
as you shine *Divine Light*
upon thy earth.

With each passing day,
your *Divine Essence*
shall guide the way
to *everlasting love* and grace,
as chaotic-negative energy
is erased.

Expressions, Purity of Love

Hypnotizing eyes,
You mesmerize me—
Seducing me with your *aura*,
Your essence—
Your beauty.

Sinfully delish

As I welcome you
Into my embodiment,
To embellish
The purity of my soul—
An empty canvas.

Lay on your essence.
Lay on your creativity.
Lay on your aura.
Allow me to be
A reflection of who you are.

Allow me to express your thoughts,
Your feelings—
In physical form.
Let me be your canvas,
To reflect the purity of *your* soul—

As you cover my surface,
With each thought.
Each line.
Each detail—
As you stroke your brush,
From one end of my canvas
To the other.

As your eyes pierce through me—
Arouse me— With your synergy.
Connect with my canvas—
My purity.

As your thoughts
Become seduced by imagination,
You pierce into my flesh.
Oils— Dripping unto my flesh.
Wet— Colorful— Cool sensations,
Carrying thoughts of the imagination,
I become—

From that of a droplet.
As you smear, oils, upon my canvas,
I lose a part of me—
My purity.
My surface— Changed.

Added to my purity
Is the energy of your soul—
The energy of your thoughts.
Your creative imagination
To make me different,
To make me an expression of yourself,
Of the depths of who you are—
Your soul.

There I felt it— Another droplet.
Another shade— Another layer.
As my canvas becomes unrecognizable,
I see you.
I see your soul, staring at me—
A mirrored reflection of your imagination.

As I embrace your emotions,
I become unrecognizable.
My purity has become ecstasy.
I've never felt this way before—
I'm loving myself.

All eyes will be drawn to me
I'm no longer a blank canvas
I Am, a reflection of life—
Painted emotions,
Human feelings,

Human thoughts,
Human imagination—
I've become—
Transformed.
Into *art*.

Final Thoughts

I shall scribe one final thought
Before closing this chapter
Of my efforts in preserving humanity,
As the *Universe* ushers in new beginnings.

May this unique collection
Serve as a reminder to
Stop Sinning!

My thoughts...
Let the Power of Love—
To bring about Love,
Be your first thought of the day.
To resonate from a voice of
Sound, mind and body.

As *Mother Earth*,
In her fertile state,
Trembles and quakes,
May she bleed new life into
Her oceans, and become
The loving potion
To wash away
The vengeance of hate;

As it cultivates
Enough negative force
To turn her tides,
Cause her pressure to rise—
Only to leave the very planet
We call home, a haven for
Demonic *Spirits* to roam,
Seeking a host that looks
Just like you.

So be cognizant of what you say
And do, as you become a reflection
Of your *Divine Soul*.

Flawless

Flawless is
My canvas;
My heavenly
Divine Earth.

As I sow seeds
Of righteousness,
To prepare
Humanity
For rebirth

Divine seeds,
Ripen—
Sweet nectars
Of my fruitful *Earth*.

Aromatic
Fragrance
Of my
Floral essence;

Divinity
Is what
You've evolved
To be

Mirrored
Reflections
Of my whole,
My beautiful,
Flawless,
Beings.

Floetry

Come with me.
Flow with me.
Come flow with me.
Let my *Spirit* excite
The essence of your soul—
To set your *Spirit* free,
As you take flight
In my essence
Of *floetry*.

Forever in Love

As my healing waters
Baptize thee
In the name of *love,*
My *Universal Essence*
Shall shine through
To your hearts and souls
From above.

As *Divine Will*
Ground your essence
To the loving soul
Of thy *Earth*—
As she nourishes the rebirth
Of humanity,
Divine Love shall forever be
Within *Earthly* hearts.

Free

Strength,
Power,
Grace,
Is what I see,
When I look into the soul
Of humanity.

My *Divine* species,
Fighting to survive,
As they attempt to thrive upon
My fruitful *Earth*.

As rebirth of ideas
Are invented,
By the advancement of
Artificial intelligence,
The soul of the human *Spirit*
Becomes dormant—

The body becomes restless,
Filled with anxiety,
As distressed energy is released,
To be absorbed within
Multi-dimensions of my
Divine Earth.

I shall rebirth your souls anew,
And shadow everything you say
And do, and not infringe upon
Your *free-will* to be,
What you were born to be…
Free!

Free Spirited Energy

Death of my *soul* awakens me,
Along my quest for *Divinity*.
Rituals— entraps my mind
As my *Spirit* and *body* intertwines
With the energy of *Mother Earth*—

The protector of my skin,
The *Giver of Life*,
Of all *Divine* creations.

The knowledge you seek
Lies beneath your feet;
Fusion of light energy;
Single ignition of the *Divine Spark*,
Whose energy never goes out;

Gaseous – Liquid – Solid,
Crystal formations of *Matter;*
Dark Matter
Light Matter,
ALL (*Life*) Matter;

She doesn't discriminate,
She loves us all the same!

Seek first within your *soul*
for the eternal flame
of the *Divine Spark*.
No meditation is required
to fuel her loving energy;
Her kinetic vibration
is in harmony with all life.

As a butterfly spreads it wings
during its journey of life,
let us learn from its *creation*;
its *mutation*— its *transformation*;

To become the *Monarch*
that we were born to be...
Free Spirited Energy

Galactic Essence

Cosmic explosion of the soul
Unfolds within,
As human nature is reduced to sin,
When it defies the nature of thy *Universe*—
The source of origin;

Love and compassion
Shall reign upon thy *Earthly Star*
As *Star seeds* of the *Cosmos*
Guide our hearts from afar;

As *Galactic* essence
Pushes the threshold
Within our souls,
Divine Life unfolds
To heal humanity of its sins
Once again.

Give Me Strength

What a waste,
My life has been;
If I reduce my suffering
Down to sin—
Down to being preyed upon,
By human suffering.

The misery of the soul
Becomes weak,
When it seeks
To prey upon the meek.

Silenced voices of a child
Cries out in the wild—
Spirits set free,
No longer entraps the vessel
That lives in misery.

Give me strength, Dear God!
Give me strength!,
Cries the angered soul—
Letting go of its suffering.
Give me strength!

Strengthen my heart,
Allow me to love again—
Do not reduce my suffering, to sin.
Give me strength!

Goddess of Divine Love

O' *Great Spirit of Hathor,*
I give my praise to you.
May your blessings be felt
Throughout the *Heavenly Universe,*
For all that you do.

Great Goddess of Fertility
and Love— You bestow to us,
From the *Great Divine;*

May the essence of your sublime love
For humanity be intertwined
Within our hearts.

We shall never part
The teachings of your *Divine* ways.
To our *Goddess of Divine Love,*
We shall always pray.

Ground Thy Soul to Thee

I hereby,
Ground thy soul
In the *Season of Love,*
For the reason
I Am to be—
To live a life
Of compassion
For the preservation
Of humanity

Universal Essence,
Ground thy soul to thee,
As I surrender my essence
To your *Divine Will*—
For my quill shall be
Forever grounded
In your *Divine Love.*

Harmony

Flow as one with my
Universal harmony,
Give of your freewill
With just one dance with me

Dance in my essence
To the natural rhythm
That you were born to be,
An instrument upon my Earth,
A conduit for my Divine Universe,

As my cosmic planets align themselves
With my beloved *Earth*
I shall energize your souls
With the *Spirit of Love*
Upon *her* rebirth;

As she reciprocates *her* love
To the *Divine Universe* above,
To *all beings,* below,
We shall bestow,
Peace, love, and harmony.

Hate and Strife

Sing with me,
Chant with me,
As *Divine Energy*
Synergizes our soul—
Unfoldment of thy *Universe*.

Dance in song
With the *Divine*
As *Universal Love*
Comes to life,
To conquer the entity of
Hate and *strife*.

Hate, Rest in Peace

May the *Spirit of Hate,* forever
Rest in Peace!

The *demons* that once
Circled thy *Earth,*
Would not let us sleep.
All day long,
They chant in songs,
As their vile souls weep
Of pain.

Stained, teardrops.
Stained, bloodshed.
Divine Entities,
Trapped—
In a dimension of time.

Their *Spirits*
No longer entwined
With thy essence—
Tormented souls
Guided
To the *Divine Light* of *Love,*
In celebration of their victory.

As their *Spirits are welcomed* home
Once again,
May their service to humanity
Serve as a beacon of *Hope,*
Into the afterlife.

Heart of the Divine

Spoken from the heart and soul
Of the *Black Mother*,
Cursed upon your birth,
To share my *Divine essence*
With the *Spirit* of another.

Twin soul, of my *Universe*,
Since parted from the heart
Of the *Great Divine*—
Seeded within the core my *Earth*,
To nourish the soul of human kind.

Rooted from the core of my soul,
With each breath of your being
Cosmic energy unfolds,
As you bear the seeds
Of the *Almighty Sun*,
Sons of Great Nations shall be born.

Like the sacred essence
That nourishes my fruitful *Earth*,
Broken are the curses of another kind.
Blind— For their eyes cannot see
The cosmic rays of my *Divinity*,
As I shine my essence down on thee.

May the waters from my sacred oceans
Cleans the sins of thee—
With each breath of my air,
Take in all of me.

Re-root your feet into my solid ground;
Compound is my *Earth*, you shall rebound,
To be as *one* with my *Spirit* (fire),
To ignite your cavity—
Take flight like the phoenix
To be reborn in my *Divinity*.

Hello to Love

Self-assurance requires no validation,
It's compassion of the heart—
Spiritual appreciation,
When the beloved soul
Requires no standing ovation.

It's when the energetic being
Of humanity is in synchronization
With the soul of the *Divine*,
Who entwines all life forms
With the *Great Spirit of Mother Earth,*
As she gives rebirth, to you—

So let go of the ego and say hello to Love.

Higher Good

Destruction of the soul
Begins within,
When you open your vortex,
And invite in *Sin*.

When humanity rejects the teachings
Of the *Great Spirit,* she will begin
To cleanse her auras
Of unwelcomed entities
That does not serve a *higher good*.

She's not to be misunderstood,
Or abridged to a mathematical equation;
For she aligns her essence with *All*
Persuasions— From *Black, Albinos,*
To *Caucasians* alike.

She relies on her *Indigenous Tribes*
To help her thrive— As she provides
Plentiful, for us to reside *peacefully*.
In harmony with the essence
Of the *Divine Universe.*

History is No Longer His to Tell

Delicate String of Life—
As I lend my chord
To the cosmic vibration
Of the *Divine Universe,*
As her cosmic sound
Resonates throughout her galaxy—
Emitting wavelengths of *Divine Love;*

As her frequencies stretches
As far as the human soul can feel—
When reality becomes real
And love becomes the energy
That manifest with each thought
The *Spirit* creates;

As the *Divine Universe*
Absorbs the energy of hate
From the evils that controlled mind creates,
History is no longer his to tell.

How to Mend a Broken Heart

Love is the melody
Of the harmony I play,
When I break the cadence of hate.

Evil is, what evil creates.

But in a *world of peace,*
You must surrender to the *good will*
Of a more kind and gentler heart.

For hate— Once torn apart
From the whole of its other half,
Will inevitably surrender to *Divine Love.*
The healer of all sins.

Human Evolution

Finally, I can breathe,
As my eyes awaken to reality.
Time no longer stands still
As *Human Evolution*
Pushes the threshold of *freewill*.

Waiting on the other end
To tame the *free spirit*
Of *Cardinal Sin*
Are catchers of the *Spirits*
That take flight—

Along their plight
To capture the essence
Of the human soul,
As *Divine Life* unfolds
Within the soul
Of humanity.

Human Race

Do not be in a race
To rush through life,
Before graduating from the
University of Human Origin.

Do not pray to an *Icon,*
To forgive you of your sins.
Take responsibility for your actions
And learn to forgive yourself,
With just a simple breath,
By repeating the words…
I Love Myself!

As often as it takes
To convince your *Spirit*
That the *Universe* made no mistake
When you were seeded
In the *Essence of Divine Love*

I AM, Life

Fertile seed of my essence,
I give birth to you—
Divine Life, of my halves;

Masculine is my protection,
Feminine is my yolk—
Conjoined, in perfect union
as *one,* fertile seed.

Each cycle I bleed,
to nourish my fertile womb—
In harvest, you lay, until *conception.*

The perfect union,
I bring to life, to live as *one*—
Upon my fruitful earth.

Upon birth of my *seedlings,*
I introduce you to
the *Spirit* of my *Divine Universe.*

GOD, as *I Am* called.
For *I Am,* all things.
I Am, *Life.*

I AM, the Universe

I AM many things,
   And many things
Are of me.
   I AM all things,
And all things
   Are of me.
I AM the sacred core
   Of the human soul,
Through my *Divine Spirit*
   All life unfolds.
Through one's life journey
   My tales are told;
Rebirthed seeds
   Upon my sacred Earth,
As I give rebirth
   To Angelic life—
Broken are the curses
   That harbors human strife,
As souls conjoin to become one,
   Under the *Divine* light
Of the *Sun,*
   My crescent *Moon*
Shall nourish the souls of thee,
   As I take root
In thy holy ground—
   My compound *Earth;*
As she rebirths
   With the kindred *Spirt*
Of the *Universe*—
   Love and unity
Shall be her blessing
   To humanity.

I Bestow, Love

No thoughts, rhyme or reason
Comes to mind, as I cleanse thy earth,
During the *Season of Love*
From above, to all realms below,
I bestow love, within thy Earthly hearts;
Tis the season to be jolly, as happiness renders
The soul complete—

As the cosmic cycle of love is complete,
I bequeath my heavenly angels
The duty to sacrifice at will.

As my quill is laid to rest,
For I have done my best—
I shall soar throughout the *Universe*
Until my season arrives again;

To cleanse thy *Earth* of sin,
As humanity's heart is reset once more,
And *Divine Love* is restored.

Indigenous is My Soul

Native is my *Spirit*.
Indigenous is my *Soul*.
May the *Divine Universe* unfold
Her *Loving Essence*,
To bring forth revelations
Of *her* existence—

To heal the soul of humanity,
And put to rest the insanity
Of a once scientific mind—
Whose institutions has *raped*
Nearly every inch of thy
Sovereign Earth.

A *Lover's Creed*, now broken,
By the desires of *greed*, that feed
Upon the hearts of her *Indigenous Tribes*.
Conquer not, a humbled mind.
Conquer that of the beast
That has manifested within
One's own heart,
To be delivered from sin.

Centuries ago, torn apart,
From the *Loving Essence*
Of thy *Sunlight*, that melts away
The peaks of thy bosom,
To deliver riches downstream,
To patch the womb of her divided *Earth*.

For humanity's worth,
Is of more value than any weight
of gold, or its silver lining
that threads her broken heart.

Black Seeds of her melanin tribes,
Has nourished her nations,
Since the creation of time.

All *Akashic records*
Speaks of the *Divine,*
When strife did not exist
In her heavenly worlds—
Only Love, which is cradled
In the bedrock of humanity.

Death be to insanity
That breeds hate upon itself
As the flood waters shifts,
And balances the oceans
Of the Heavenly *Universe*.
Humanity shall celebrate
All of her *Divine* riches,
And the *Spirit of Love* shall be
The first order of business of the day.

I Set You Free

I rest my head on the shoulders
Of the *Divine Universe,*
As she releases her hold
On the *free will* of humanity,
In her moment of forgiveness…

"Why didn't you do it sooner?!"
Are my thoughts, as I remain at *peace*
In her moment of silence—

While humanity attempts to defy
The *laws of gravity, Karma* shall greet us
At daybreak, as the *Universal Will*
Of thy Universe, sets us free,
To become *saviors* of ourselves,
And be held accountable for our
Sinful actions. We shall no longer cause
A chain reaction of emotions, as humanity
Continues on its path of *self-destruction.*

I Surrender My Free Will

I *Surrender* my Free Will to, *Love*
I *Surrender* my Free Will to, *Peace*
I *Surrender* my Free Will to, *Joy*
I *Surrender* my Free Will to, *Hope*
I *Surrender* my Free Will to, *Happiness*
I *Surrender* my Free Will to, *Compassion*
I *Surrender* my Free Will to, *Compromise*
I *Surrender* my Free Will to, *Serenity*
I *Surrender* my Free Will to, *Humanity*
I *Surrender* my Free Will to, *Unity*
I *Surrender* my Free Will to, *Positive Energy*
I *Surrender* my Free Will to, *Balance*
I *Surrender* my Free Will to, *Mother Earth*
I *Surrender* my Free Will to, *the Universe*

If I Do More, I Go Farther

If I do more… I go farther in life.
This is the motto I live by.

If I do more with my mind,
I go farther in life.

If I do more with my hands,
I can build things— I go farther in life.

If I do more with my body,
I can accomplish anything.

If I do more with my energy,
I can light the path for others to follow.

If I do more… I go farther in life.

In Jesus' Name

Children of thy *Universe,*
I call upon thee,
Receive all that *I AM,*
Divine Energy.

Waste not!
Want not!
In my realm,
It's all the same

Call upon thee,
To absorb your pain,
When you give praise to
My *Holy* name.

For thee, *I Am,*
Above— *Infinite love,*
As your energy
Pours into my soul,
Divine life unfolds.

Layer upon layer,
Is where I begin;
Fragments of my
Essence exists within.

As skin is to flesh,
As is your *Spirit*
To my *Divine Soul;*

Conjoined within
my *essence*—
Your *sacred abode.*

My name,
Is your name,
In my realm
It's all the same.

As I rescue you
From yourself—
Once again,
In *Jesus'* name.

Infinite Universe

Surrender your essence to me,
As my *Spirit* beckons
Your warm embrace.
Twin souls, conjoined
at the heart of the *Universe,*
when you gaze upon my face.

Pools of oceans between us,
As our lustful foreplay begins.
Subtle thoughts of eroticism,
Fuels the passion of our sins.

Welcome to my *Queendom*,
The den of all desire,
Where fantasy fuels
The imagination of the flesh—
The soul of the *Universe's* fire.

Our lustful passion quenches
her thirst, upon delivery
of her light— Kinetic explosion
of her soul— Where all life unfolds.

With but a glimpse,
I take you there,
Along my soul plane
To the *Great Divine*.
My zenith stretches far beyond
My black heavens, where
All life intertwines.

Come soar with me,
Beyond my infinite heavens.
Make love to me this starry night.
As infinity syncs all souls
With the *Divine Universe,*
As we climax to become whole.

Void,
Space,
Matter,
All movement,
Stops.

As she resets and balances
The *Sands of Time,*
As new life ferments within
The Earthly womb
of the *Great Divine*—
Twin souls, intertwined.

Injustice to Mother Earth

An injustice to *Mother Earth*
is a threat to all of her creations!
When the vibrations of the *Universe*
echoes through to the human soul,
she beckons you to surrender
your *free will* to the *Divine Spirit,*
to awaken your heart to *love.*

Rebirth of the soul is *infinity.*
It has no beginning or end.
It is what it is— *Infinity.*

The science of nature co-exists
within the soul of all living beings,
created by *Mother Earth's* great
alchemic design, to outlive humankind,
as the naked eye remains blind
to her majestic ecstasy.

Invitation to Life

Come walk with me,
Says the *Universe,*
as she extends
her warm embrace,
as her timeless essence
shines upon your
angelic face—

Embodiment of
her infinite life,
all life intertwined.
She does not
count or measure
the degrees of time.

Energy flows
wherever she goes,
still is her movement,
as if there's nothing there,
she is everywhere.

All life co-exists
within the womb
of her *Divine Earth,*
upon rebirth
of her alike kind,
your eyes are blind
to thee;

As she envelopes
you in her bosom,
to walk hand in hand
with *Divine Energy.*

Justice for All

Crimes committed against humanity
Shall be forgiven,
As the forbidden
Fruit of Knowledge
Nourishes our souls within.

For the *Laws of the Divine Universe*
Has weighed in—

Let us be cleansed of
Our past transgressions
As we vow to evolve
To commit lessor sins.

Yet preying on the minds
Of the *meek* and *compassionate*
Is an unforgivable sin
Which is why complete surrender
Of the *Free Will*
Allows *Earth* to reset your heart,
Again and again.

Karma

The *Divine Universe*
exists within our skin,
in the sacred cavity
of the soul.

Hollow shell,
where *Spirits* dwell,
gateway to eternal life.

Earth, their haven,
vortex to the afterlife—
To be recycled, again,
and again.

When life begins,
rebirthed souls will either,
live a life of sin, or as *Spirit Guides*,
you decide— your *Karma*.

Lady Evening Star

As I step into your glorious light,
I see reflections of my
Shining armor.
I wear it loud and proud,
As I vow to never harm you.

Lady Evening Star,
No matter where you are,
I will defend your honor—
Beyond the skies of heaven,
To the infinite *Universe* above.
As you grace us with your presence,
The essence of *Divine Love*.

Lava

My compound *Earth,*
Release your hold on me,
Allow my *Spirit* and *soul* to breath,
As thy heavenly waters
Soothe my pain.

Rain down on me,
Universal Love,
As the skies above
Reflects rainbows
Of your delight;

Remnants of my lullabies,
As your crystalline vibrations
Soothes my somber cries,
As thy *Divine Universe*
Rebirth my soul,
Again and again;

As I burn away
Humanity's darkest sins,
Peace and *love*
Upon thy *Earth*
Shall be restored,
Forever more.

Laws of Nature

You do not have to be *forceful,*
When the *Laws of Nature*
Does not cater to your *Will.*
Be patient.
For the gentleness of *Love*
Always circles back around again,
At the precise *Divine* moment
When you can appreciate it.

Life's Challenges

Don't underestimate yourself,
by overestimating yourself.
Life is full of challenges,
with pitfalls along the way.

Before you seek to conquer
your destiny, get a lay of the land;
Connect with nature, *Mother Earth's*
natural environment, and let her
Spirit guide you along life's journey.

Like Dust, You Rise

Have my words
Not taught nothin,
To escape the wrath
Of your own demise—
From the sizzlin heat
Of the bayous,
Into the musty air…
Like dust, You rise.

Broken chains;
Rusted shackles;
Decayed plantations;
Politicians lies—
The only sweat that drips
From your tired lions,
Lies in-between your thighs.

Sister-girl— Boyfriend,
Twisted mind,
Long good-byes;
Spirits long forgotten
Shall lift the veil
From your weary eyes.

Music industry;
Sporting industry;
Corporate Industry;
It's all the same—
Branded since your birth,
Destined to live a life
Of public shame.

Don't point the blame
At your massas,
Who themselves
Live in shame—
Exploiting the profits
Of your labors,

As you bask under
Their iridescent lights,
You call fame.

Showcased in their
Mass arenas,
Where the matador
Confronts his whore;
What's left is a blood sacrificed,
Unearthed from the ocean floor.

As empires rise, and fall again,
Guilt is your only sin,
As human life is recycled,
To repeat itself,
time and time again.

Love Orbits Evolution

Resurrected within my soul,
    LOVE

Seeded within my heart.
    LOVE

Emitting from my being,
    LOVE

An expression of who *I Am*,
    LOVE

Evolution of Humanity,
    LOVE

LOVE Orbits Evolution.

Loving Blessings

Loving blessings, you are to me,
Rain down abundance upon humanity.
Plentiful is your fruit, as we re-root
Our souls to the core of *Mother Earth*;

Rebirth our souls in the *Spirit of Love*,
From the *Galactic Universe,*
Above— Below— In-between;

As you reenergize our essence,
May our likeness— Be of your likeness,
May our efforts— Be of your efforts,
May our love— Be of your love;

May our *Spirits* be filled with *Peace, Love,*
Unity, Tenderness, Compassion and *Grace*,
For all of humanity.

Luna Moon

O' Divine Lunar Moon,
Today I give my praise to you.
I'm thankful for your essence,
And all that you do.

My shining light,
Who comforts my soul at night;

My shining star,
Who protects my soul from afar;

My *Solar Essence* above
To whom I reciprocate my love;

You are the *Divine* essence
Who silence my seas—
My heart stands still
When I become one with you;

My Earth,
My Sun,
Has risen this day.

I steady the way
To make room for you,
To protect my *Spirit*
In all that I say and do;

For thee *I Am*— *I Am*, You.

Make Love, Not War!

As reality of *human evolution*
Settles in, to reveal centuries of
Blasphemous sins,
My mind is no longer blind
To the atrocities that veils
The heart's emotions—
As the vigorous entities of hate
Swells within the sediments
Of the oceans—
And the *Divine Universe, rebirths*
Her soul, *Anew.*

Milky Way

Immeasurable, is my infinite light,
Said, the *Universe,*
As her *Divine Essence*
Breaks through time and space.

What's the matter?,
As artificial matter, shatters
At the sound of my voice.

   Abort!
   Abort!

Your alternate course of action,
As I create a chain reaction
Throughout my *Universe*—
As the nebula of my *Milky-Way*
Shines bright like never before.

Misunderstood

To understand the entity
Who gives their lives to thee,
Is to understand those
Who stand for *liberty*.

To understand the entity
Who lives for *Peace, Love* and
Unity, is to understand
The unconditional love
For thine *Beloved Mother*—
In the eyes of the *Divine Universe,*
There is no other.

As we bow down
And give praise to the *Great Mother,*
Who bore the seed of thee
Almighty Man—
The one who raises his head
To the sky,
So he can better understand
The true nature of his *free will*—
The day the *earth* stood still;
To allow him to better understand
Himself.
Protector of the Divine Universe.

Moral Duty

When you walk along the path
Of *truth* and *righteousness*,
You have a *moral duty*
To uphold the natural laws
Of the *Divine Universe*—
To live in harmony with *Mother Earth*,
And bestow love and compassion
Towards others, during all
Of her *harvest seasons*.

Morning Delight

Your moon-rays dances
Across my pillow,
Shadowed reflections
Of your *Divine* essence;

All day long I think of you,
As you envelope my soul
With glittered reflections
Of your morning delight,
My crystalline waters
Absorbs all of you.

As night falls, in my dreams
I'm reunited with your *essence;*
I awaken to your smile;
To your morning delight,
To your sweetness,
To your joy—
To your unconditional love.

My Spirit Yells

Deliver me from hell,
as my *Spirit* yells,
somber cries for freedom.

Held in captivity
of misery, as truth is
reveal to me.

> *Lies...*
> *Lies...*
> *Lies...*

Untold truths,
and evil sorcery, governs
modern-day society.

Illusions— Programmed souls.
Remotely controlled
by technology;

To quench the thirst
of corporate greed—
As they feed upon your soul.

Reality, forces my eyes to see
the *cardinal sins* of humanity,
as human nature reveals
itself to me.

Do I dare resist temptation?
The whelms of sorcery,
that forbids your eyes to see
the light?!

Look within, to guide your Spirit
back to the *Divine* light,
to be reintroduced to your *Divine*-self,
which harbors the reality, of *Love*.

Natural Beauty

Mirror, mirror,
On the wall,
For I shall not befall
To life's insecurities.

For vanity shall not weaken me,
To the point of insanity—

Pure and natural, I shall be,
As the essence of thy beauty
Reflects the purity of the soul.

From my heart, love shall never part,
As the *Divine Essence of Love*
Becomes my creative work of art.

Natural Essence of the Universe

Each time I *breathe in*, and *exhale*
The *Natural Essence of the Universe,*
Love and *Happiness*, are the blissful words
That comes to mind, while creating a *New Me.*

Reborn Spirit, in the natural realm,
Where *source energy* co-joins *All life* forms,
To thrive in harmony with our beloved
Mother Earth, and her *natural essence.*

Natural Hair

If my momma don't like her *natural hair*,
Why should I like my *natural hair?*
Your hair is nappy, my momma said.

When I became of age,
She did not dread the day
That she could use a hot press comb
and straighten out my *natural hair,*
Or use a CHEMICAL RELAXER.

But today, I have a choice,
To wear my hair
In its own *natural* way.

Not wigs, locks,
Or weave extensions;
Fabricated— Artificial
Plastic hair.

My hair is beautiful!
My hair is coily,
Like the roots of *Mother Earth.*
My hair is natural!

I was born with this hair.
My hair defines me.
My hair allows me to be *Free,*
Which is what my *natural hair*
Means to me— *Free!*

Not Upon My Flesh

Not upon my flesh,
Shall your words
Pierce through to my soul,
Seeking to satisfy the desire
Of your *cardinal sins*.

Not upon my flesh,
Shall I welcome you,
As your words seek to seduce
The very essence that protects
The sacred chambers of my abyss.

Dare you attempt to steal a kiss,
To penetrate through to my heart—
My oceans torn apart
When *Earth* brought forth ecstasy
To cool the passion of her soul,
As *Divinity* unfolds.

I shall guard my flesh!
I shall not weaken my heart
To your fleshly desires!
Not upon my flesh,
Shall you prey!
I rebuke you this day—
Not upon my flesh!

Pain Shall Exist No More

Pain…
Release me from your hold,
As the *Essence of the Divine* unfolds
Within, to cleanse thy soul of sin—
Your agony shall exist no more!

As I welcome the *Divine Energy of Love*
To resonate from my heart,
My connection with the *Divine*
Shall never part—
A joyous smile greets me
Each day, as her healing resonant
Brings positive energy my way.

Through the *art* of my quill,
I shall surrender my *free will*
To the energy of *Divine Love,*
As her loving grace stimulates
Harmonic vibrations of thy
Universe above— Who shall
Forever soothe my anguished soul.

Peace, in the Wake of Evil

As the *Feminine Essence* rise,
To its own demise,
Evil is as evil does—
As the *Divine Universe*
Silence its thunder
To bring forth *love*.

In our world
We create.
When she gifted us
With the seeds of life
It was no mistake.

In the hearts and soul
Of every man, woman
And child, Love shall
Nourish our union,
from the *Great River Nile*.
As the nature of Evil
Is left to ferment
In its own hate.

Peaceful is My Earth

Delicate is my skin,
For I shall cleanse
Thy flesh of sin.

Love abound,
Clouds fill the air,
Raindrops everywhere.

Delicate is my soul,
As new life unfolds
I shall strengthen the whole.

Peaceful is my *Earth*.
Nourished,
The life of rebirth.

As my loving essence
Fills the air—
Rebirth everywhere.

Play

Imagine if we played all day
In the open air
That nature brings,
When our hearts sings
Of joy— Oh boy!

I would want to stay
Outdoors all day,
To enjoy *Mother Earth*,
As she envelopes my soul,
To feel the joy and love
Of the good life—

Where life is as blissful
As smelling the roses
In the *Spring,*
Picking a dandelion
In the *Summertime,*
As the *Autumn* leaves
Wanders about—

When the harvest
No longer sprouts,
As the essence of *Winter*
Brings a quiet moment of comfort
To reflect upon the beauty
That *Earth* brings to life—
As the hearth of the fire
Warms our hearts
With memories of yesterday,
As we played, in her vast delights.

Power of Desire

Love— adorn me.
Envelope me
With your grace.

Rain upon my face,
Divine essence
From your heavens.

Within my soul,
I shall embrace
All of you—

Water
Earth
Air
Fire

The embodiment
Of thy *Universe*,
Who inspires me
With the
Power of Desire.

Praise

I AM, healthy.
I AM, strong.
I give birth,
All day long—
To new cells,
As they grow,
Positive seeds,
I must sew.
To receive
Good blessings,
I must believe.
I must not practice
To deceive.

There are good
And bad people
In this world,
Who prey
On the minds
Of little boys and girls.
A child's mind
Is pure and meek,
And is vulnerable
To the weak.

I must say strong
All day long.
With others,
I must get along.
The *Power of Love,*
Is in my heart.
From my daily prayers,
I must never part.
No weapon
Shall penetrate
My protective space,
As old habits
Are erased.

I shall surrender
My *free will,*
To receive
The Universe's
Loving energy,
Which is the love
She pours in me.
I shall give praise,
And trust in me.
I must believe
In Love,
To receive.

I AM, healthy,
In Love.
I AM, wealthy,
In Love.
I AM, *Praise,*
Fulfilled!

Protector of My Soul

As you envelope me
in your warm embrace,
I shall erase
thoughts of my bad,
for goodness sake.

Protector Moon,
not a day too soon,
you have arrived
this starry night.

As your heart shines bright,
Protector of my soul,
as new life unfolds
I am forever thankful
for all that you do.
I Love You.

Queendom of Love

Don't try to control, *it*,
Or *it*, will control you,
This things we do, called
Star Girl Majic.

Just simply breathe and receive,
As *Unity, Peace* and *Love,*
Becomes the vibration
And calibration
From above.

Simply ground your feet
Upon thy *Earth,*
To be rebirthed as
Divine Seeds of Life—
Where strife does not exist
In her heavenly *Queendom.*

Raw Emotions

I am a virgin to my own thoughts.
Purity are my actions. I bask in a sea
of purified waters.

Cleansed of human sins.
Cleansed of human nature.
Cleansed of human thoughts,
actions and emotions.

The curiosity of *Earthly* life
excites my free will
to explore boundless possibilities
beyond *Cardinal Sins*—
To experience *raw emotions*.

For I am but a soul,
yearning for the gentle touch
of a pure heart.

Yearning to be cradled
in a sea of *Divine Love,*
where I surrender my free will
to the seduction of raw emotions—
Where my actions are spell bound.

I surrender my all to you,
for one night
to bask in your oceans.

Where I'm under
your hypnotic spell—
Captivated by your charm,
Your *Divine Essence,*
Your *Divine Beauty,*
Your *Divine Love,*
Tonight, I'm yours…

Rebirth of Divinity

I center myself in your likeness
as your *Divine Essence* unfolds,
to replenish my etheric being
that brings new life to my soul.

Like the lotus that grows
on your sacred mountains,
the purity of your infinite fountains
revives my sacred abode.

*Within each cavity of thy Earth
infinite life rebirths, Divinity.*

Receive Me in Kind

Embellished
Within my soul,
Divine Truth,
That unfolds
All the sins
Which has sough
To lay their wrath
Upon my *Divine Earth*,
And forces me
To rebirth
Thy souls
Anew—

As I prepare
Her seasons to
Receive me in kind,
The *Collective Spirit*
Will no longer
Be blind
To thine
Divine Light,
Who shall forever,
Deliver your mind
Through the perils
Of darkness,
Into the union of
Divine Love.

Relax

Why be in such a hurry
There's no need to scurry,
To become engulfed in the fast lane
Of modern-day life.

Take it easy and breathe,
When things get to hectic,
So you can simply relax
And avoid misery and strife.

Rest in Peace

Hidden beneath
The ugly veil of hate,
Is a wretched soul
In need of a hug;

Love is the energy
Transmuted,
When two worlds collide
In the human stratosphere;

The calming sensation
Of thy *Universe*
Shall absorb all pain and misery,
To put old issues to rest.
So she can rest, in peace.

Resurrection Day

Resurrection Day,
I must say,
Following behind the herd
Of *free will* thinkers
Has led me astray,
From the *intuitive light* within.

Divine Master,
Cleanse thy soul of sin.
Forgive me now
For my transgressions—
The aggression
Of thy soul
Has become weak,

Like the meek-minded
Who has become blinded
By the fallacies the magi's
Have created,
As their victories are celebrated
On the New Harvest *Moon.*

Goddess Lunar,
Not a day, shall you arrive
To soon—
Shine your essence
Deep into my heart,
For I shall never part
From your *Divine* whole—
As the *Sun's* delightful essence
Soothes my tempered soul.

Sacred Waters

Sacred Waters, within thy *Earth,*
Compound to *Love*—
As Above,
I shall ignite
The passion of your
Divine Spirit—
To nourish the soul
Of humanity—
To carry out
Thy *Divine Will*
As my essence flows
Through your artisan quill
To guide your heart
To Divinity.
Infinity—
Your ultimate destination.

Salvage thy Earth

Must I stand before you,
To repeat myself again—
What part of, *thy shalt not kill,*
Did you not understand?

You insist on building
More weapons of mass destruction,
And yet to halt your mass constructions,
To cover every surface of my earth.

Soon, I will have to give birth
To a new civilization
Who will not defy me,
Or seek to control humanity—
For the purpose of greed.

I shall cleanse thy *Earth,*
As my tides rise high.
Soon you will say good-bye
To your norms, as my wrath
Brings forth my natural storms—
To salvage thy *Earth*, once again.

Save My Soul
(Dedicated to the legacy of Dr. Stephen Hawking)

As my *Spirit* cries out
To the *Divine Universe*,
Save my soul from the chaos
That I've created, as new *theories*
Are being generated
To prove that one *theory*
Is more advanced than another.

Mother Universe, free my *Spirit*
From this wicked curse,
As time is set to go in reverse,
Set my *Spirit* free, from the
self-destruction of humanity.

I am but a brilliant mind,
Who was able to escape
The confines of society,
To explore my own reality,
To aide in the enlightenment
Of like-minds to come.

Sun, as I come before you,
To praise at the bequest
Of your almighty throne,
My *Spirit* shall no longer
Roam thy *Earth*.

Rebirth my soul into the cosmos,
A place where the average mind
Is afraid to go, as I explore regions
Far beyond your galaxies.

I fear not what is yet to come,
As I rise to the *Glory* of the rising *Sun,*
As your *Moon* shines into my *soul,*
To guide the light into the darkness
Of your vast *Universe.*

Self-Destruction

Divine Universe,
Temper my heated soul.
For I have become easily angered
By hate which has become the norm
Of the energy humanity creates.

We live our daily lives basking
In human suffering,
And the plight of human existence
Is headed down a path of
Self-destruction;

Fueling the energy of
Chaos and fear— With no clear
Solutions to heal our minds of hate,
But would rather gravitate
Towards the negative energy
Our thoughts and actions stimulate;

To guide anguished souls
Back from whence it came—
The core of the *Divine Earth,*
To be rebirthed
In the *ecstasy* of her desire;

Thus fueling the energy
Of her cosmic fire—
As *Divine life* unfolds within,
Evolution of the soul
Shall heal our minds of sin,
To nourish the seeds of
Divine Creation.

She Sustains Me

Mother Earth provides for
My primary needs.
She sustains me.
She gives me a planet to call home,
And allows me to have love in my heart
For all humanity.

And guess what,
She doesn't require much in return.
All she asks for is recognition
And respect for humanity,
In the name of *Peace,*
Love, Compassion, and *Unity,*
Around the globe.

Silver Lining of Hope

Darkness prepares me for you,
The *silver lining of hope.*
When all is lost
I think of you.
I day dream of you,
I become you—
Sunshine on a rainy day.
Rainbow in the sky.

When the *hope* of
Love and surrender
Brightens my day,
A ray of your love
Shines within my heart—
Delivers me from darkness,
My thoughts
No longer torn apart.

Be the silver lining in my sea of love.
Be the silver lining in my sea of hope.
Be the love to my shining light.

Deliverer of love from above,
My hopes and dreams comes true
When I think of you,
I love you.

Sins Against Humanity

When is it going to end?
Violent-sins against humanity.

Voices cry out…
"Stop I can't Breath!"

Voice cry out,
What have you done to me?!"

Voices cry out,
"Stop Freeze!"

Fear…
Fear…
Fear…

Fear for survival.
Fear from genocide.
Fear from extinction.

The vast bubble we call *Earth,*
Welcomed us upon our birth.
Recycled into a world of sin,
As violent atrocities against humanity
repeats itself again, and again.

But what is fear without love?
What is love without compassion?
What is love without hope?
What is love without love
For humanity?

Soul Healing

When the *Divine Universe*
Survives you, from an ailment
That has caused your *soul*
To endure *pain* and *suffering*,
You will be ordained
By the *Divine Universe*,
To serve a *Higher Purpose*,
In guiding others
Along their journey
Of *Soul-Healing*.

Soul Mate

Deep within your magma,
I lay to waste,
Broken, from your
Fragmented core—
Combustion of *solar* love
From the *Cosmic Universe* above.

Catastrophe collisions
Of all dimensional times.
New Beginnings.
Endings.
New life.

I burn in the heat
Of passion, as your
Thermal fusion attracts
Star seeds from afar—
To nourish you.
To pleasure you.
To soothe your
Tempered soul

I awaken to your ecstasy.
I awaken to rebirth.
As your *Spirit* soars
The *Cosmic Universe,*
In search of, your *Divine*
Soul mate.

Soul of Compassion

The *unconditional service*
To *humanity,* is a *kind deed*
Never complete,
And a path less traveled.

A new path, we must pave,
To guide others
To the *Soul of Compassion*,
Along our evolution
Of humanity.

Soul Wealth

We should have our
Next conversation
In *Heaven,*
When our *Divine Spirits*
Reflect upon
The times we spent
Living our current lives
In the *fast lane*,
Trying to keep up with the
Mundane issues,
Plaguing modern-day society.

The abundant rewards of life
Is time spent
When each moment
Should be a conversation
About *good health and good wealth*
Of the overall
>*Spirit,*
>*Mind,*
>*Body, and*
>*Soul.*

Not a material possession to achieve.

Soul Wealth,
Are treasured moments—
That lives on
To infinity.

Sound of the Universe

I carry the *Sound of the Universe,*
Her voice sings through to my soul—
Harmonic vibrations of *truth,*
Untold!

Simply close your eyes…
Feel her pulse,
As *Divine Truth*
Unfolds within—
As the cosmic resonance
Of the *Universe,*
Cleanses our souls of sin.

Energetic sensations—
Divine calibration,
To receive the essence
Of her mystery,
As our senses realign
With the essence of *truth,*
To feel the reality of her
Divine history;

Universal Essence of all around
Compounds thy *Earth,*
As she rebirths *Divine Love*
Into the souls of humanity.

Sovereign Queendom

Black Indian is my *Spirit*.
Copper is my skin.
To trace the linage of my ancestry
Is to date my essence
To the origin, of humanity.
When nations thrived
And cultivated in harmony
With the *Divine Universe.*

For I was not born, or raised
On a plantation-reservation.
My essence does not conform
To the manifestation of *hate*—
That's become the dominate
Source of energy
Modern-day society creates.

Conceived in Love,
GOD made no mistake
When she decided to replicate
My *seed*, in the *Spirit* of her likeness.
To serve as an instrument,
For the *Divine,* to help nourish
The *enlightened minds*— To thrive
Within her *Sovereign Queendom.*

Spirit of Hate

When the *Spirit of Hate*
Attempts to tower
The *Spirit of Love*,
The *Divine Universe*
Destroys its very foundation.

The fragmented pieces
Of its abhorrent soul
Are consumed within
The star gates of thy
Earthly Universe—

To be cleanse and rebirthed
Into a more *Loving Being*,
And be of *higher service*
For her *Divine Will*.

Spirits Take Flight

Mother Earth, I hear your cry,
As you awaken my soul at night.
Spirits Take Flight, carrying your
Harmonic *sound* in the wind—

Your gentle breeze, beneath their wings.
Angels take flight, like fire flies,
Reaching the height of the horizon,
They sing and dance their rituals of *love.*

"Ignite my fire," they say, as they begin to pray
Over thy *Earth,* joined in a *circle of love.*
High above the horizon, reaching the zenith
Of the *Universe,* their energy of love abound,
As they carry her cries within their wings.

> *They sing…*
> *They shout…*
> *It's Spring!*
> *It's Spring!*

As new life begins to sprout from thy *Earth,*
Beauty brings its own mystery, as fire burns
From her soul, her truth unfolds, as she welcomes
New birth upon thy earth, as the loving energy
From the *Universe* rains down love unto her
Sacred ground.

Love is in the air.
The *Spirit of Love* is everywhere.
"We shall become loving Human beings,"
The angels sing, *"Let there be love,*
Let there be light from her oceans."

Her potion to heal humanity,
The Spirit of Love.

Spirits of the Underworld

As a pebble is thrown
Into my waters,
My *Divine Essence*
Ripples through
to your soul.

As the energy of love
Unfolds, *Spirits* carries
My essence
In the wind.

As love comes ashore
Once more,
My *Earthly* nature
Shall reunite with
Spirits of the Underworld,
As they awaken to explore
My heavenly creation.

As human temptation
Desires my forbidden fruit—
The likeness of the *I Am*,
My *Divine Essence* shall be
Introduced to your soul.

Spoken Word Poetry

I'm in love

With Poetry.

Poetry is me.

I'm in love

With myself.

I'm but a

Verse,

Waiting

To be

spoken.

Surrender

I hereby surrender to
The *Spirit of Darkness*,
As your kinetic energy
Lures me beneath your veil;
Fragmented pieces of reality
Composes your life in hell—
Mirrored reflections of illusions,
Is what your misery foretells;

Let us dance this starry night,
As our energy breaks through
Heaven's veil— Rebirthed
In the likeness of the *I Am,*
our energies compound
Thy *Earth;*

Rebirthed flames of lust,
Passion— *Hell's desires*
Fulfilled within all living beings,
No longer living in delusion,
As truth becomes reality.
As love rebirths within our souls,
May we become whole this starry night.

Survival of the Fittest

When *GOD* introduces you
To real pain— True *Love*
Is what you will gain,

When you survive the grief
Of a heart strained,
While battling the *test*
To do your *best*,

In a realm where
"Survival of the fittest"
Is the biggest joke
Amongst the tricksters,

Who uses spells
To foretell their fate,
Instead of taking ownership
Of the evil they create—

Living a life of sin,
One must repent
To be rebirthed again,
By the power of *Divine Love*.

Sweet, is the Fragrance of Love

Divine Universe,
Envelope thy essence
With the fragrance
Of *love*.

Let *love* greet me
Each morning
With its sweetest aroma,
To brighten my day.

Let *love* be the incense
Of my meditative state,
To excite sacred dimensions
Of my eternal being—

As I receive all of you,
In pure form,
As my ecstasy rise
From your delightful aromatics;

May the quintessence of your *love*
Soothe my tempered soul at night,
As I dream of your delights
And awaken to the sweetest
Fragrance of your *love*.

Temper Thy Soul

As *likeness* is to me,
Divine Energy
Pours into thy soul;

My *Divine skin*—
Akin to the soul
Of the *Universe.*

Science cannot define
The essence *of*
Divine Energy,
through its use of
Artificial intelligence;

As it declares
Electronic warfare
Upon thy *Universe,*
May her wrath
Be tempered.
Praise to the GODS!

The Abundance of Love

Purity of the Soul shall manifest,
When *morality* and *hate* aligns
With *Love* and *Compassion*—
Their everlasting strife is forced
To agree to unity, when *Divinity*
Cleanses all celestial bodies
Of thy *Universe*—

When curses, *are broken.*
When misdeeds, *are forgiven.*
When the mind is driven
To the brink of insanity,
Morality is there to pick up
The shattered pieces
Of the *Divine Heart*—
Universal worlds torn apart
By *anger, lust* and *pain.*

I shall bestow upon
Thy *Earthly Universe, Love.*
Blessings from the *Galactic* realms
    Above,
    Within, and
    Below.

The Abundance of Love
Shall be the harvest
Of thy labors—
For the pain brought about
By a hateful soul.
All is forgiven
In my *Divine Queendom.*

Love shall be the *Creed*
To evolve humanity,
As *World Peace* and *Unity*,
Unites *All Nations*—
Torn apart by the perils of *greed*.

Greed, shall no longer
Corrupt the soul
Of thy *Earthly* nations.

Greed, shall no longer divide
A *Sovereign Mind*, on matters
Of the *Divine Heart*.

Greed, shall no longer fuel
The passion of hate!
May it Rest in Peace.

The Almighty Sun

Close your eyes and imagine
The *power of love*
Pouring into your heart…
Close your eyes and imagine
That your *soul* and the *Universe*
Will never part…

As your *Spirt* sings a song of
Rejoiced emotions,
It shall become *one*
With the radiance
Of the *almighty sun*.

Close your eyes and feel
Its loving sensation,
Knowing that your
Compassionate work
For healing humanity
Is never done!

The Art of My Essence

Poetry,
The Art of My Essence,
As *Divine Love* comes to life.

With each stroke of my pen
New thoughts begin,
As the *Divine Universe*
Heals my heart of sin.

Not from what I've committed,
But from what I've admitted,
After bearing witness to
Humanity's strife.

For truth is the notion
Of all things,
As the potion
Of lies sings
Through to the soul
Of the *Universe.*

With each verse
I've spoken,
Her *Divine* wisdom
Becomes a token,
To deliver *Love*
Into our hearts,
Once again.

The Gift of Life, is Love

I'm *awakened*.
As the *Essence of the Divine*
Flows through my oceans—
Igniting my magical potions
To fulfill your every delight.
Be the *Sun* to my *Moon*.
The *Moon* to my *Sun*, at night.
As reflections of *Divine Radiance*
Glows across my seas,
Exciting the very best in me—
Illuminating my heart's desire.

Oh, what love we make.
We were destined to become One.

I meet you here again,
Under this starry night.
Our passion explodes
In a *Sea of Love*—
Reflections of who we are.
Reflection of my Earthly Star.
Reflections of the Divine.
Reflections of all life, entwined.
Reflections of One Soul.

As we rejoice beneath the glory
Of the *Divine Universe*,
We create a new story
In the *Great Book of Life*,
On the eve of rebirth—
All curses broken.
All negative emotions
Released.

As we become ONE,
Once again,
Our souls cleansed of sin.

As we ground ourselves
To the *Universal Cord of Life*,
We give birth to New Life.

As we receive her *Divine Essence*,
We shall become her Divine Essence.

As we receive her *Divine Protection*,
We shall become her Divine Protection.

As we receive all that was meant to be,
We shall become ONE.

From beneath her seas, *I rise.*
I rise above it all.
From beneath her seas,
I shall tell a new story.

Beneath her seas is, *Divine Life.*
Infinite *sands of time.*
Beneath her seas, lies my
Sacred tomb of life.

My waters, protect me.
My waters, heals me.
My waters, nourishes me.
My waters, provide for all that *I AM.*
My waters, ground me.
My waters, balances me.
My waters, preserves all things.

Beneath my crystalline oceans,
Lies the soul of *Mother Earth*—
Sacred Root of Divine Life.

We shall be nourished once again.
We shall flourish once again—
As new foliage grows within you.
Grows outside of you.
You are the foliage.
You are the Divine *Tree of Life.*

As you rebirth yourself anew,
With each breath you take,
You sustain yourself—
As your soul is nourished
From the essence of my oceans.
My sacred potions—
My *Sea of Divine Love.*

As I rain down love,
To quench your *Divine* thirst,
I shall give you but a single droplet.
For life begets life.

As I replenish my oceans,
I shall nourish your rebirth.
I shall absorb your hate.
As you recreate a better version
Of *Your-Self*—

> *Your Beautiful-Self.*
> *Your Magnificent-Self.*
> *Your Omnipotent-Self.*
> *Your Divine-Self.*

As you live on for centuries
To come—
As you become
> *Timeless.*
> *Ageless.*
> *Infinite.*

You shall be the *Sage of All Times.*
You shall absorb my loving energy,
All that I have to *Give— Divine Wisdom.*
For *I AM* the infinite *being,* within all *beings*—
The *Divine Darkness* and the *Light.*

As I preserve the sacred seeds
Of the *Tree of Life,*
Divine Union of the Soul
Gives birth to L*ove.*

Love, it what it is…
The *Gift of Life*.

The Menagerie of Life

Enter at will,
Through the artisan of my quill,
As I perfect my skill
To balance the essence of
Truth and *Universal* wisdom;

As the masses, dangles
From the strings of their
Puppet masters—
As their lives face disaster,
While they hold on to dear life,
At the distress of corporate elitism—

Big pocket bankers,
Aka "Corporate Gangstas,"
Old money— *New money*
It's all the same,
In a realm where the stakes are high;

But before it's declared *game over,*
Souls will be called forward to die,
To test the skills of another—
Brother *against* brother,
Mothers *against* mothers;

What's left is but a hollow shell,
Left to dwell in a realm of hell—
Playground for the wicked,
Soul-less *Spirits*.

The Perfect Union

The *Divine Universe* did not make
No mistake, when it decided
To create, the *Masculine*
And *Feminine* essence;
The living quintessence
Of *Itself.*

Conjoined, to live as *One*
Whole, where either half
Shall become bold
To dominate the being
Of other—
The *Divine* extension of thy
Father and *Mother.*
The *Perfect Union.*

The Universe Shall Speak

The *Universe* shall speak,
As our souls are in concert for *Justice,*
Peace, Love, and *Compassion*
For humanity.

The *Universe* shall speak,
As our hearts beat
To the same rhythm— In sync,
As *One.*

The *Universe* shall speak,
As our souls are conjoined—
In the name of *love.*

I shall speak for the *Universe*—
The *Universe* has spoken!

The Veil of Hell

The *Veil of Hell,*
Shall foretell
The wicked evils
Of sorcery—
As flying objects
Reaches the zenith
Of the horizon,
The *Universe* shall
Greet them with a smile,
On a job *well done!*
As the sun breaks way
To guide the light
Far beyond
Her *Earthly star.*

Thrive

Oh, how the *Great Spirit,*
And *Soul,*
Has become separated
From the *mind* and *body*—

Torn apart from *Divine
Human nature,*
Which lives in harmony
With the *Divine Soul.*

Once whole,
Upon thy *Earthly Universe,*
Made half,
By *destructive forces;*

Now, broken pieces,
Shattered fragments
Of thy *Earthly* heart.

She shall mend your wounds
As her *Divine essence*
Is made whole—

As you thrive
Upon thy *Divine Earth*,
Once more.

Today's a New Day

Today's a new day,
Hallejuah

Today's a new day,
Let us sing

Today's a new day,
Hallejuah

Today's a new day,
Let us shout

Today's a new day,
Hallejuah

Today's a new day,
Let us praise

Today's a new day,
Hallejuah

Today's a new day,
Let's not doubt

Today's a new day!

Twin Flame

As you gaze into my eyes,
I'm mesmerized.
Entranced in love,
I'm hypnotized.

As you stare into
The pit of my soul,
Galaxies, no longer
Amidst us—
Vulnerabilities,
Exists no more.

No more *oceans*
Between us, as my
Loving energy
Comes ashore.

For you are the *Earth*
To my rising seas,
The better half of me—
As *fire* burns, within
Our *flame of love;*

Your *Air,* carries me
To the *Black Heavens*
Of the *Universe,*
Where thy eternal flame
Ignites the starry skies.

When I return to *Earth,*
You embrace my
Infinite being,
As rebirth of thy *Spirit,*
Gives new life to my
Divine soul.

Umbilical Cord of Life

What was born in us,
Will always be a part of us.
For we are simply tiny particles
Of the infinite *Divine Universe*.

Cosmic seeds of
Crystalline matter—
Divine Light,
That will forever shine
Upon *Earth's* heavenly canvas.

Spiritual ties unbroken,
To our umbilical connection to
Mother Universe,
And her vast wonders.

Unfoldment of Divine Love

As the essence of my pen begin
    To dichotomize the human soul,
Divine Love unfolds, within—
    With every stroke of my essence;
Be it my voice, or whatever craft of choice.

I'm simply a *devout scribe* of modern-times,
    Helping to balance the *sands of times,*
As the *Spirit of Love* intertwines itself
    With the manifestations of hate—
The energy of what an angry *Spirit* creates.

We must learn to make *love* and procreate
    New seeds of *Divine Life,* and nourish them
With every ounce of our being,
    Foretelling from what the soul
Of thy *Universe* is seeing—

That humanity is but a breathe away
    From self-destruction.
Yet as the essence of *Divine Love* ignites
    A combustion within our hearts,
Her *love* for thy *Mother Earth*
    Shall never part.

Universal Essence

Children of thy earth,
as you seek rebirth
of my *Universal Essence*,
allow my *Divine Spirit*
to reawaken your soul.
As my *Divine Energy*
infuses every fiber
of your being—
Your neurological
chord of life.

Religion is merely con-text,
written to distort the mind,
to blind your senses
from rediscovering
the truth that lies within
your soul's center—
Your sacred chamber,
which nourishes your heart,
as you lay protected
inside your mother's womb.

Seek not to follow the path
of another man's journey,
to find the true essence of you.
Look within, to break the spells
of the mythical tales
of man's original sin—
Feel the ether rising
in your *Divine Soul,*
as *Truth* awakens you to see
the light that you were
burn to be— *Free!*

Universal Guidance

Galactic wonders,
My eyes have seen,
Majestic remnants
Of thy Queen;

Crystalline fragments
Of the *Great Divine,*
Whose mysteries
Stretches beyond
The measure of time;

Space and matter
Embodies her essence
Of *truth*— Where illusion
Is mere fantasy;

Reality, is her existence.
Awakening, is her resonance.
Love, is her compassion
For humanity;

As her energetic vibrations
Guides lost souls to rediscover
Who they are— May they find refuge
Under the guidance of her *Universal Stars.*

Universal Stars

As I embrace the *Divine Essence*
Of all around,
I ground my *Spirit*
To the *Soul* of thy *Earth*.

Rebirth of *Universal Stars*
Shall form in unison,
To guide new *star seeds* to
Entwine with the *Divine Soul*
Of humanity—

As strife between love and hate
No longer questions what I create.

I shall awaken thine eyes
To not be blind
To thine internal light *(plight)*
Of the human soul—

As *Galactic life* unfolds
Like the seed of a lotus,
Your *Universal Soul* shall blossom
The beauty of *Divine Love*.

Vow

Scribing for the *Divine Universe*
Has been a pleasure,
The wisdom that I've received
Is beyond measure,
It has brought enormous
Enlightenment to my soul.

Before I grow old,
I shall fulfill my true desire
To encourage and inspire
The hearts and minds
Of humankind.

As I look upon thy *Earth,*
Beyond the veil that covers all life,
I vow, not to lend my gift
To perpetuate chaos and strife.

Love is my frequency.
Love is my vibration.
My service shall be for the salvation
Of the humanity—
Not to aid in its self-destruction.

We Shall Evolve in Love

Love shall evolve in all things,
As humanity's soul is reset
To live in harmony with the *Divine*.

These precious moments in time,
Shall be a remembrance of
How far we've come,
And how far we have to go
To achieve *Love, Peace,*
Unity and *Goodwill* towards
Our fellow humankind.

May compassion be restored
Into our minds and hearts,
As it becomes the first honorable
Act of the day.

We Shall Rise

Washed upon my shores
Once more,
The evil entity of hate—
I shall not surrender
To your destructive will,
And allow you to procreate.

Humanity shall not submit
To your demise,
For the *Energy of Love*
Shall rise;

We shall live together as *One,*
Under the protection of
The *Moon* and *Sun*— Our work
To the *Divine Universe*
Is never done!

When I Hear Music

Music is my religion,
As it resonates from the
Sacred chambers of my soul.
Like the petals of a lotus,
Divine melodies of the *Universe*
Unfolds— When I hear music.

Chords of *Divine* life.
Drums, Beats, Rhythm.
Divine sound, all around.
Delightful melodies
That natures brings,
As I rejoice and sing
A song of freedom.

Liberation of my soul.
Earth tones.   In synchronicity
With the *Universe,*
As her heavenly beauty unfolds.
In an orchestra of *Divine Love.*

White Beauty

Purity of the soul,
Reveals itself
In your light.
Shine your essence
Upon my darkness,
Deliver me into the light.

Purify me.
Balance me.
As I become whole.
My Yang to my Yin,
As thy Earth
Is delivered from sin.

Why Does My Genius Offend You?

Why does my genius offend you?
Would you rather I do cart-wheels,
Or swing from a tree like a monkey?
Yet your scientific *studies,* relates
the monkey to be our cousin.
Possessing the same genes as humans.
Known to mankind, as the most intelligent
Of our species.

Again,
Why does my genius offend you?
Would you rather I stand like a statue.
Even then, I will be most admired.
Exhibiting the master craftsmanship
Of the world ingenious artisan.
Molded from the elements of
Mother Earth's most delicate clay.

Why does my genius offend you?
Is it because of the color of my skin?
My high-melanin skin—
Said to possess the most ingenuous cells
In the human body, for its *GODly* abilities,
Not yet proven by mankind.

Again,
Why does my genius offend you?

X-Rated Soul

Do I dare stand before you,
To bare the purity of thy soul?
Stripped down to my bare flesh,
To be paraded in my *birthday* suit.

But what is there to celebrate?
As I'm auctioned off
To the highest bidder,
Who will celebrate
In the richness of my worth,
Of my deeds—

Whether I sow his seeds,
Plow his fields,
Or bear his next generation—
Massa will never understand
That I'm still a woman,
Unashamed to bare
The purity of thy soul.

You Are The Power

You are the *Compounds* of my *Earth.*
You are the *Fire* of my *Soul.*
You are the *Ocean* of my streams.
You are the *Depths* of my whole.
You are the *Air* life brings.
You are the *Desires* of my dreams.
You are the *Power* of my *Universe.*
You are my *Everything,*

Zeal

The zeal of your appeal
Excites my essence to thrive,
When I think of you
My *Spirit* comes alive.

Twin flame of my *Universe,*
Guide my pathway to the stars,
From afar, we shall inspire humanity,
As we become the *Flame of Love,*
That we were born to be.

Soulful Expressions

"If *GOD* built the *Earth* in *6-days*, how long did it take to build the *Cosmic Universe*?"

"I'm a firm believer in *Truth*, whatever *"Truth"* is."

"If people spoke *Truth*, before speaking a lie, the world would be a safer place."

"Why is history being repeated— Rather than being taught accurately?"

"To understand your *true nature*, is to understand the nature of the *Divine Universe*, and its mysterious-infinite wonders."

"It is within man's nature to go beyond curiosity— As he reaches the brink of self-destruction; while his mind continues to explore new advances in technology."

"When the *Moon* absorbs and balances the energy
of the *Cosmic Universe*, she nourishes *Mother Earth's
Etheric Soul*, with love and *compassion for humanity.*"

"As the ocean replenishes our rivers,
the *Divine Spirit* replenishes *All* life forms."

"Humanity is in dire need of *moral calibration,*
before it *self-destructs."*

"The *moral compass* that calibrates the *human soul*
is the *Spirit of Love.*"

"The *Divine Universe* awaits, to align its frequency
with the *Loving Soul of Humanity*— Don't keep her waiting."

"Allow *Love* to be your companion, instead of *Hate*—
Misery is always in search of a soulmate."

"Love is the frequency of the *Universe*—
Become *one* with its choral essence."

"Love ignites my passion, and grounds my *Spirit*
to the core of *Mother Earth*, as her frequency reflects
the essence of the *Divine Universe.*"

"Dance with me. Sing with me—
To the joyous melodies of *Love.*"

"Close your eyes and ears to hate,
and open your *soul* to *Universal Love.*"

"The *Power of Love* affords personal freedom to say
whatever the soul desires, in the *Name of Love.*"

"When the *Spirit of Air* ignites the passion of *Love*—
You give, and receive it, in abundance,
with each breath."

*"Love expresses *compassion* and *virtue* of the collective soul, and resilience for preserving humanity."*

"When I lift the *veil of hate*, all I see is the *Spirit of Love.*"

"Can you imagine, *Peace, Unity* and *Love,* throughout our *Earthly Universe?...* I can!!"

"When you open your heart to receive *Universal Love*— The *Light of Compassion* shines through."

"There are more important issues in life to discuss, such as, the *Power of Love*, and the preservation of humanity, rather than lending your energy to *hate* and *greed.*"

"Attune your frequency to *Love*, to always be in harmony with the *Divine Universe.*"

"Lend your emotions to the positive energy of *Love*,
not to the negative caprice of *hate*."

"It takes a *special person* to devote their lives to caring
for *Mother Earth's* special animals—
May they be blessed with *Unconditional Love!*"

"When the *Spirit of Hate* is quick to anger the mind,
only the *Essence of Love* can soothe its tempered *soul.*"

"What is true *Love?*...
To be in *harmony* with the *Divine Universe.*"

"Learn to *Love* in this life,
you can always *hate* in the next!!"

"*Love* is the synchronistic vibration of *All* living beings,
resonating in harmony with the *Divine Universe.*"

"Love is the *soul-root* of happiness that was first seeded
by the *Divine Universe,* upon creation *of Mother Earth."*

"Flow, in the delightful *Essence of Love,*
to make for a positive outcome, in tough situations."

"Humanity is one big melting pot
of the Essence of the Universe, conceived in *Love."*

The *Essence of Love* is my shield,
to repel the negative forces of hate.

"Let *Love* be the *natural remedy* to cure the body's ailments
of hate!!"

"The *Power of Love* carriers the strength of the *Divine
Universe,* through unconditional *acts of kindness."*

"Stand *strong* in the *Spirit of Love*—
Not *weak* in the *Spirit of Hate.*"

"Like the *Phoenix*, the *Power of Love* ignites passion
within the human soul, to *Rise* to any occasion."

"When you release the dead weight of *hate*,
Love propels your heart to *soar* like an *Eagle!!*"

"To live and have never *loved*, is like you've never lived
at all— Live life to the fullest, in the *Spirit of Love.*"

"*Love* is the communal frequency of the *Divine Universe*, and
All living matter— Surrender to its *will*, to bring about *Peace*
and *Harmony* throughout the human race."

"Ground your essence to the soul of the *Divine Universe*,
to receive and reciprocate *unconditional love*,
during the *Cosmic Mating Season.*"

"Internal *Peace*, *Love* and *Compassion* for humanity,
lies at the core of *Mother Earth's Cosmic Universe.*"

"Receive *Love*. Become *Love*. Evolve in *Love*."

"*Love* is not an emotion felt, but an emotion shared—
In the *Spirit of Compassion.*"

"Why does humanity feed off the negative energy of
greed, fear, chaos, and *hate?* When *Love and Compassion*
creates a more positive and harmonious environment."

"Grounding your thoughts in the *Serenity of Love*,
lends to happiness, and a better quality of life?!"

"Pray for *Love*—To *balance* our emotions. *Heal* our pain.
Cleanse our souls— And ultimately achieve *World Peace*!!"

"May the *Spirit of Love* inspire compassion within our hearts, while our *higher service* to humanity be of *Loving* Grace."

"While the human resolve is being tested on a daily basis— Sow seeds of *Love* each season!"

"It's less tension on the heart to celebrate the *joys of life*, in the *Spirit of Love,* than suffer in the *misery of hate.*"

"When the collective soul humanity *awakens* to the *Spirit of Love*, we will embrace *World Peace.*"

"What if *hate* was a trend of the past, and the *Celebration of Love* becomes the *New Movement of the Day.* To unify humanity, once and for all."

"Don't be an enemy of *Love*, when it comes in *Peace.*"

೭ळ

"America needs a hug! With a strong dose of *Love!*
To cure its *infectious culture* of hate."

"As a *Free Spirit*— My *faith* is guided by the *Divine Universe*,
in the *Essence of Universal Love.*"

"As a *living being*, the notion of a *human race*,
is what it is… A *Competitive Spirit*, fighting to survive."

"Imagine, *Unconditional Love* throughout *humanity*.
I can."

"It's not nice to infringe on the sacred rituals
of *Mother Nature*, during her *Cosmic Mating Season*—
As she *syncs* her *Loving Essence* with the *Soul of Humanity*."

"Carrying the dead weight of anger, in a *greedy* and
miserable soul, leaves no room for *Love* to grow."

Love sees no evil. *Love* sees no hate.
Love sees only *Love*.

Anchor your heart in the *Essence of Divine Love,*
to allow *positive energy* to flow through to your mind,
to shield you from the perils that plague humanity.

It takes more energy to *hate* someone
than it does to *Love* them— *Unconditionally.*

Center your soul in the *Essence of Love and Compassion.*
And see how swiftly the *Divine Universe* responds in kind.

Karma… The hazards of life.

As we reflect the energy we *create—*
Let us *unify* in *Essence of Love,*
and not *magnify* the forces of hate.

Pain and *tragedy* has a way of soothing the tempered soul
of humanity, by bringing about *Unity, Peace* and *Love*.

In the eyes of the *Divine Universe— Mother Earth* has evolved.
Human nature takes on an evolution of its own.

Hate kills *Unity—*
The teachings of Divinity teaches us,
thou shalt not kill.

Be in harmony with the synergy of the *Divine Universe,*
as Love becomes your vibrational frequency— Not hate.

As a *Free Spirit, Love* is my frequency— Vibrating in
harmony with the *Essence of the Divine Universe.*

What if… "*Americans,* put more energy towards *Love* and
Forgiveness of our ancestors' *transgressions*— Instead of
repeating the *Dark Ages* of the past."

When the problems of the world weighs heavily
on your soul... *Retreat!*

"Acts of Compassion, in the Spirit of Unconditional Love,"
makes a stronger impact on a person's life,
while strengthening the *soul of humanity.*

Prejudice and hate, was so last Century!...
Get with the times and evolve
in the *Essence of Love."*

Karma is nothing to fear, as long as
your heart is filled with *compassion.*

As your *soul* seeks a *cult,* or *tribe* to belong,
let the *Essence of Love* be your *culture.*

When you let *Karma* serve its purpose,
it is always *sweet* in the *bitter* end.

Let the *Essence of Love* be your *Karma,*
to emit positive vibrations throughout the Universe.

Karma is like a looking glass,
reflecting the consequence of your intentions,
before putting your thoughts into *E-motion.*

The *Universal* vibration of *Love,* harmonizes
with all living beings, attuning our minds and hearts
with the soul of the *Universe.*

Karma—
What goes up, must rebound…
To teach lessons in life.

The Ultimate Black Out… Silence, in still waters.

What if…. *Americans* boycotted the media,
and electronic digital services for a day?...
That will be something worth gossiping about.

When you open your heart to receive *Universal Love*, the
energy is so strong that it bonds your frequency to *hate*,
to celebrate, in the *Name of Love*.

Hate is like *misery*. Always seeking a companion,
to dwell in its own misery.

Be a positive instrument to the *Divine Universe*,
not her enemy!!

Why complain about something, if you are afraid
to take a positive step forward to change the situation.

There is nothing new about the *news*,
simply a repeat of negative events!

Is constant *negativity* being forced into our system
to make us immune to it?!

I was warned, years ago, to never lend my energy
to politics or religion, for obvious reasons!!!
It's mentally and emotionally draining!!

The non-stop rhetoric of politics and religious feuds,
is becoming more and more brainwashing.

Religion... "*Ancient* experience,"
to guide you through *modern-day* life."

Heaven, is a peaceful state of existence,
not a *place* you go after death.

"Do you believe in *Love*?," should be asked,
before asking, "Do you believe in the *Bible?*"

Love is a sensation you feel,
that requires no explanation of its origin.

People need to pray more, and protest less!!

When you surrender to *Divine Love*,
you will discover *GOD's* grace for humanity

Soul Love, is seeded and nourished by *Mother Earth*—
in the Spirit of creating *Universal Love*,
Peace and Harmony.

What if everyone prayed for *Love* and *Peace*,
at the same time around the *world?*
For just that moment, we would achieve *World Peace*.

Hate pours into the soul of those
who profess to be more superior than the *Universe*.

Don't preach— Teach.
Sing and dance— Don't yell and shout.
Praising Love and being happy, is what life is all about.

Earth has multiple dimensions, within multiple dimensions.
Each with a soul of its own.   Like the many species
that inhabit her— *all* interconnected to the same *source energy*
that nourishes the *Universal Soul of Mother Earth*.

Watching constant negativity from *"news"* events,
kills more brain cells than lithium ions
from cell phone batteries.

Which is worse, negative *news* or *social media?*
You guessed it… They both like to stir up hate!!

In a world filled with chaos, it's easy to be bad,
than good!

Blessings be unto those who speak of
the *Universe's Divine* work, to carry out *goodwill*.

Let *Compassion* be your *Frequency*,
and *Love* be your *Vibration*.

What if Americans boycotted hate, prejudices and racism for the rest of their lives?.....

When the *frequency of Love* taps into your soul, surrender to its *Divine Will*. To resist, will only cause *pain, misery,* and *regret*. For not recognizing that it was part of you all along.

The only *slavery* I know is *modern-day slavery* guised by conglomerate industries!!

Now is the time to pray for *World Peace*, not make threats against humanity!!

Mother Earth's love for humanity thrives off negative energy— She can absorb your thoughts before releasing your body into action.

Slavery is no longer a *state of being*— It is a *state of mind*!!

Stay centered in the *unity* of *Peace* and *Love*,
to balance the polarities of *Good vs. Evil.*

To carry the weight of the world's burden in our hearts,
is a burden in and of itself.

We must learn to "*Relax, Relate and Release...*" To bring
abought *balance* within all realms of humanity.

Peace begins when you detach your *Spirit*
from the insanity that has morally corrupted humanity!

It is easy for *world leaders* to make violent threats into a
camera— To bring harm to citizens of other countries,
instead of promoting *Love, Diplomacy* and *World Peace*!

Watching the *news* is worse than chemotherapy and
radiation treatment— All are toxic
to your immune system.

*Darknes*s would rather pull you into its darkness, rather than allowing your soul to be rescued by your *Divine* loving light.

Dark and light energy measures the same in the *Cosmic Universe*— *S*he gives *Love* equally.

Nature will heal you, if you let her.

Love is a religion for the heart. It requires no membership, tithing or church service. Just simply a belief in the *Power of Love*.

The negative emotions of *fear* and *hate*, shackles the mind and body, thus perpetuating mental slavery!! Break free of the shackles, and soar to new heights.

When it comes to life… "Believe in all things, but believe in nothing." Until you have personally experienced it!

When you ground your *Spirit* to *Mother Earth*
she will bestow unto you, all the blessings of the *Universe!!*

The modern-day mind is like *Bermuda grass*— *Artificial*.
And will eat nearly everything *natural,* in its path.

Fruitful blessings be unto those who care for *GOD's*
children, with a caring and giving heart!!

If you don't have self-love, or family support,
don't expect for anyone else to fully support
your endeavors in life.

Let *Love* be your *frequency* and *instrument*
to carry out the *Will of the Divine Universe*,
which requires only 1% of your natural *essence*.

Close your mind to negative *new*— Trust me,
your body will thank you later.

To liken your heart to a man's soul
is to liken to *Divine Love.*

Fire, Earth, Water and Air—
All loving elements of the *Divine Universe.*

Hate is dead energy, reigniting itself—
Fueled by negative human emotions!!!

Why does the *news* always promote negativity,
such as "hate, war, and violence," when *Love*
is a better topic of conversation.

GOD designed you with a brilliant mind.
Yet it is easy to allow others of lower intelligence,
the power to control it?!

The Spirit of Hate is like a pebble thrown
into a quiet pond— Once it makes contact,
it changes the *natural laws* of balance.

Love and Compassion expresses the strength
of the collective human soul.

From every *Seed of Hope* flourishes a brilliant mind.
Plant positive thoughts into the minds of others
and watch it thrive.

If you are busy competing in life, you won't have time to stop
and see the beauty of the *Divine Universe*.

When the perils of life test your patience— Let Go!,
and let the *Divine Universe* fight your battles.

Hate does not apologize for itself.
It is its own entity that will defend itself
as much as *Love*. At some point,
we have to call a moral truce.

Soul Love, is the power to surrender
to something greater than yourself.

Don't be in such a hurry that you forget to breathe.
The nourishing *Spirit of Air* is a breath away.

DO NOT TAKE what you want in life—
Earn it!! When you put your best foot forward,
the *Universe* rewards *in kind*.

Search within your soul to find the keys to unlock the door
to *source energy*, on your journey to achieving *Success*!

The path of righteousness is a path less taken.
It's just a foot-step away.

When you teach *wisdom* in the name of the *Wholly Spirit,*
all sacred knowledge is revealed by the *Divine Universe.*

Gravity propels Greatness.
When you play to *Win*… You have already have *Won*!!

Life is a journey of the *soul,* and a path *you choose.*
If the trail is already paved, *widen the road.*
If you choose a different path, *either direction,* will lead you
to the same *Destination. Reincarnation of the Soul.*

To *Make America Great…* We must celebrate
The Spirit of Love. Not perpetuate the *Evils* and *Hate*!

Just the thought of *Love,* sounds poetic.

Evil only invites negative *Karma*
into your vortex, when all is lost.

Nothing will exist in our Earthly *Universe,*
if *the Supreme Creator* did not create it,
for the betterment of humanity.

When *Universal polarities* are out of balance,
positive and negative *entities* will always find
a medium to co-exist.

Humans will either self-destruct, or save themselves
from the perils of their innate nature!!

I guess you didn't read the manual,
"No Weapons formed against US shall prosper!!"
<u>#PreserveHumanity</u>

Be better than the last man standing.
Be the last *Woman* standing!

Words we seldom use, are a words we seldom feel—
Love, Peace, Compassion, Unity, Joy and *Grace.*
As we seek to achieve a more *harmonious* human race.

Live life beyond limitations, as a *Free Spirit.*

All wisdom spoken by the *Divine Spirit of the Universe*
shall one day be revealed to humanity,
in the *Essence of Love.*

Be the *Golden Thread* to the *Silver Lining of hope*.
As humanity welcomes *Universal Love* into our hearts.

Life is to be treasured and enjoyed. Not destroyed
by the advancement of greed, tyranny, and hate.

Freedom of the Mind starts with releasing your *Spirit*
from the grasp of negative energy, that stifles the soul,
from soaring the *Universe,* like the stars we were born to be.

Love is the *Divine Power of the Universe.*

It is our duty to be in harmony with the *Mother Earth,*
and preserve her ecosystem from the
destructive nature of humanity.

It is within man's nature to explore beyond curiosity,
thus ignoring the crippling affects to humanity.

Humanity was not born in sin. *Sin* manifested from the
primitive nature of the human eco-system,
to prey upon the flesh and soul of another.

When you nourish your soul with *love,*
you can better extinguish *hate*
from the soul of others.

Love from a distance— *Hate* is on the loose…

Let *Love* be your vibration—
Singing the *National Anthem of the Universe.*

Do all good deeds in the *Name of Love,*
and receive *Universal Blessings* as your reward.

Show me a country not a War with itself—
I will show you a nation of *Love.*

During the modern-age of *"Fight to Survive,"*
you will ultimately be forced to become an *entity*
left to fight against *yourself*— *To thrive.*

Nourishing the *Essence* of others, begins with
proper nourishment of your own *soul!*

When you try to put together someone who is broken,
they will either heal, or you will become broken.

The *Power of Love* fuels our souls with compassion,
to aid in healing humanity.

Love is in harmony with the *Universe.*
Hate is in harmony with itself.

Don't be afraid of *Divine Energy.*
Become *Divine Energy.*
Fearless!

I put to rest the *Energy of Hate!*
I have so much more *LOVE* to give.
To humanity as a whole!

Humanity is in dire need *calibration*,
as we continue to lose our sense of morality?

When you embrace the true sensation of the *Universe,*
you will feel the auras of her *Divine Essence.*

I'm done screaming. Tears are dried. I'm going back inside.
The fight against *hate* is over!

As humanity raises its *Loving Vibration*— Don't resist!
Simply calibrate your heart to its frequency.

WARNING…
<u>*Do Not Confront Hate*</u> face to face!
Especially to appease someone's ego!!

∽৯ৎ৯

When a phone conversation shifts your *loving* vibration to *hate*, introduce the other party to *"Dial-Tone!"*

Share the positive *Essence* of LOVE...
Not the negative forces of HATE!!

If only the *Universe* could rid humanity of *Hate*...
How *peaceful* would that be?!

Hate needs *negative* fuel to exist—
And is in constant competition with *Love*.

When negative people try to steal your *joy*...
Send them this... <u>#SorryYouAreHavingABadDay</u>

When you are fighting for a <u>Cause</u>, to heal the collective soul of humanity, intertwine your *Essence* with the Divine Forces of Nature, she's much gentler on the outcome!!...
<u>#IFightForJustice</u>

∽৯ৎ৯

#*LoveConquersHate*
Say NO to hate!... And *Celebrate Love!*

The *Energy of Hate* will consume all forces in its path—
Use caution along your journey in life, and avoid it's wrath.

Love is in natural flow and harmony with all beings

When the *Spirit of Hate* is the first to greet you
in the morning... Go back to sleep!!
And *Love* will awaken you to *Joy!!*

As *Above*... So *Below*...
The energy of *Love* lies in-between.

I've absorbed so much *hate* this week
that I can now bask in the *Spirit of Love*!!
Hate... Thanks for balancing my polarities!

In the *Art of Becoming…*
I evolve in the *Essence of Divine Love.*

What drives a person to want to harm another living being—
"Fear, Hate or Greed!" Or *All* of the above?!

Love is the *Divine Cure* of the infectious dis-ease of *Hate!*

If we allow the negative forces of *hate*
to overpower *Love,*
it will self-destruct the *Divine Soul of Humanity!*

When you surrender your *Free Will* to appease the ego
of another, their *Spirit* will weaken your heart, and cause
disharmony with the *Divine Universe.*

My Dad *Fought,* and *Stood* for *Freedom.*
I *Stand,* and   *Fight* for *Justice!!*

Reincarnation of the Divine Soul,
is the evolution of the *Spirit of Humanity*.

The more you attempt to suppress the collective
free thinking mind, the more you will invoke the forces of the
Divine *Universe*, to awaken a *New Age of Enlightenment*.

Unfamiliarity with their natural connection to *Mother Earth*,
will one day lead a *wondering soul* back to her *eternal bosom*—
To repeat the *process of life*, all over again.

Never surrender thy *Free Will* to the *Essence of Hate*.

Divine Universe, I center myself in your likeness.
As your *Divine Essence* unfolds within my heart.

As I receive *wisdom* from the *Divine Universe*,
I shall reciprocate in kind,
to nourish the *Soul of Humanity*.

Do not exhaust your positive energy
on exciting the negative forces of *Hate*.

Any threat made against the preservation of humanity,
is a threat made against the *Divine Universe*.

Solidarity of humanity, begins with understanding
the soul connection of *All* living beings.

Thrust forward in *Love*, to propel the laws of gravity
to surrender to your *Divine Will.*

Seek not to harm or destroy the *Free Spirit* of another—
Compassion of the heart reciprocates in *Love* and *Kindness*.

One's unfamiliarity with their natural connection to
Mother Earth, will one day lead their soul back to her
eternal bosom— To repeat the process of life,
all over again.

I was born a *Warrior of Love, Peace, Culture and Unity!!*
Only the *Divine Universe* can change me!!

When the *world* is in turmoil, all *Divine Initiates*
will be called forth to evolve humanity in *Love* and *Peace*.

When Divine *Darkness* meets Divine *Light* at day break,
they shall dance in unison under the rising *Sun*.

When the flesh is preyed upon, it will awaken
a *Warrior Spirit,* to avenge the soul.

When the *mind* and *body* does not accept responsibility
for its negative actions, it with point the blame
at someone else.

When the *mind* is kept discombobulated in negative energy,
it will open portals to invite in, entities of *hate*.

The Spirit of Love syncs your vibration to the orchestra of the *Divine Universe*, to always be in harmony with your *soul*.

To ignore the *root culture* of modern-day society, is to hinder the evolution of humanity.

Truth is like acid to the soul. It helps to rid the body of toxins. If your body can withstand it, you will *awaken* healthier than you were before.

The *Divine Universe* gives us boundaries, limitations, and *Free Will*, for exploration beyond the hidden veil.

When *GOD* dismisses the orchestra of *Music*, *Poetry* is left to *sing*.

When you share positive thoughts of wisdom in each conversation, the *Spirit of Love* becomes your vibrational frequency.

When the mind chooses selective hearing,
it ignores the emotions of others.

Even in darkness, humanity will never lose its *sense* of sight.
As the *Loving* radiance of the *Divine Universe*
shines into our hearts.

As *evil* treachery roam about thy *Earth*,
Love and *Compassion* awaits in the *shadows*.

Self-centeredness of the ego, needs constant reassurance,
as well as moral calibration of the heart.

When *Love* is the main ingredient—
It will always rejuvenate and nourish the heart.

Spiritual Warfare is real,
and is revealed through your senses.
Protect your vortex at all cost—
Your *soul* is what a desirous mind is trying to steal.

Life is a *cosmic*-energetic journey… Hang in there.
Soon, you will achieve *Enlightenment!!*

Do not desire to <u>control</u> the *Essence* of another—
Foreplay is simply what it is.

Don't let the polarity of doubt get you down.
Think positive!!
To shift your mindset for better results.

The *Soulful Essence* of the Divine *Universe* resonates
through all walks of life.

The depths of the human soul stretches far beyond
Infinity— *The Sacred Wisdom of the Universe.*

A decayed soul is worthy of being nourished by the *Divine*—
In a *loving* and *peaceful* environment.

Love is not a word to flaunt about.
It is an *emotion* that is interchangeable
with human *feelings* and *desires*.

For a *mind* becomes weary, when the heart is teary—
Yearning for the nourishment of *Love*.

Dance in unison with *All* living beings,
as the *Divine Universe* sings a song of harmonic
melodies, to soothe our tempered souls.

Internal warfare of self-emotions
weakens the soul,
to be in conflict with that of another.

The human soul is yearning for *Love*— *Not hate!*

For whomever profess to know what ails a *grieving soul*,
shall be the bearer of *Love* and *Compassion*.
Not the cloak of wicked sorcery.

When *Mother Earth* cleanses her *Spirit*
of negative entities— She guides the human soul
to experience a *Love* and a *Peaceful* state of mind

The more you <u>frack</u> *Mother Earth's* dimensional existence,
she will build-up enough pressure, to ultimately resist
Human Will... It's called *Karma!*

You must *expand* your mind, to understand
the journey of the soul, during its reincarnation of life.

Is it possible for mankind to *teach us* what the
Feminine Divine has allowed us to *Master*—
The *Art* of giving birth.

All Lives are vulnerable to the desires of the ego.

When *love* and *compassion* is challenged by *greed* and *hate*,
it will cause the *Free Spirited Mind* to use extreme warfare,
to protect the collective soul of humanity.

When the *Cosmic Universe* aligns itself
with the *Soul of Mother Earth*— *She* conducts her
natural selection, to test the *strength* of humanity
as a whole.

When you *fight* to resist the seductive *entity* that seeks
to control you— One day it will grow tired and weary,
and will ultimately *surrender* to your *Divine Will*.

I surrender to the *Veil of Love*. I spread my wings, *Above*.
Within *All,* in-between and below, I bestow, *Love*.

As delicate and delightful as the sweet nectar of her *Earthly*
fruits, are the *loving compounds* that nourishes her hearty *Soul*.

I apologize… if my *Vibe* is making you uncomfortable!
I'm on a different frequency…
So flow with me.

Reciprocal Loving Energy… Is just that.

Weakness is *nourished* when you *surrender*
your *Free Will* to the *desires* of another—
Strength will *flourish* when you *resist*.

Greed is an entity in and of itself,
which feeds on the desires of another.

During each phase of *Human Evolution, Love is* refined,
as our souls are entwined with the *Divine Universe*—
During its *Cosmic Evolution*.

Anchor thou *Essence* in *Divine Love*,
to receive *Universal Grace*.

Life is beautiful.
Life is as precious as a smile on a rainy day.
Life is everything… *Life is Love*.

When your mind is at ease,
you can feel the pulse of the *Universe*.

Determination of the *mind,* is the strongest *gift* of all.

Divine Love flourishes with each season,
as the *Cosmic Universe* nourishes *Mother Earth,*
during its *galactic* mating season.

When you celebrate the joys of life
in the *Spirit of Love,*
it is less tension on the heart,
than to dwell on moments of *misery.*

Be a *Seed* of *Love*— Not a *Fruit of Hate.*

As a *Free Spirit,* my mind is often troubled by
disillusioned entities, seeking to govern
my *Divine Sovereign* existence.

Love shines from the heart,
as its *Essence* envelopes humanity.

When you ground your *Essence* with the *Divine Universe,*
her *Creative Spirit* shines through.

When the *Universe* is being calibrated…
Humanity must be still, and silent!
The more *Love* she receives…
The more she gives.

Guilt wears its own shame.

"Don't surrender to the *Flame of Hate*—
Be the *Flame of Love.*"

Hate is easier to recognize than *Love*,
it wear its emotions on its sleeve—
Ready to roll up and fight.

At the end of the day, the *Spirit of Love* surrounds me.
As it expels the chaotic vibration of hate.

When you attempt to erase ancient history,
and rob it's sacred temples, it will once again flourish
in our modern lives.

When the *Spirit of Glory* is left to sing,
the *Most High Angels* chime in.

When the *Sins of Religion* is brought before
the tribunal of the *Divine Universe,*
the *Soul of Humanity* shall be cleansed, at last.

Divine Seeds of Creation, return to thee, *Delivered!*
From the *Wrath of Hate.*

We live in *2019.* *Hate* should have died last century!

When the *collective soul of humanity* unite
in the *Spirit of Universal Love,*
Peace on Earth will be achieved.

Young *Spirits* are the oldest *Souls* living among us, to keep humanity evolving— One generation at a time.

The *Fruits of Divinity* nourishes the *seeds of life,* to cure the *Spirit, Mind, and Body* of strife.

During moments of passion— Be better than your last word spoken, or last action taken.
Be the guiding light of *Love and Compassion.*

Sooner or later... Hate will be put to rest, as the *Spirit of Love* is rebirthed into *the Collective Soul of Humanity!!* WE are what WE create!!

Love... Peace... Unity is what I stand for!!
Meanwhile, *HATE* can R*est in Peace!!*

"When the Universe Speaks to the Soul of Humanity...
I Listen!"

No matter the weather…
Family needs to stick together…
Not come together,
When it's time to put a rose on a grave!!

LOVE is *Unconditional*…
It doesn't ask for anything in return!!

Love, is simply a reflection of *Love.*
Resonating from your *thoughts, words* and *actions*—
To become a reciprocal force of your environment.

Be the *Sunshine* of someone's heart…
Not the *Darkness* in their dreams!

To digest *Absolute Truth,* requires a palatable *mind.*

Duality of the heart, shall never part *Divine Wisdom.*

Before you allow someone's negative *E-motions*
turn you upside... Share *Compassion* and *LOVE*...
To turn a frown into a smile!

The non-stop competition within the *Human Race*,
will ultimately lead to the self-destruction
of the *Human Race*.

Let's continue to build bridges... Not *Walls,* or barriers!!

The only method to my madness is *Love*,
and preserving the *collective soul* of humanity.

Loving Light, balances the *Soul of the Universe*,
as she balances the *Soul of Eternal Darkness*.

Negative environments presents opportunities for
positive change, as long as you have the desire
to change your environment.

When you try and mend *someone's broken heart*,
they will either uplift your *Spirit*, or *break it*.

Instead of being a conduit of *hate*,
let your words and actions serve as a token of *Love*.

If you are not positively *developing* our youth,
you are *killing* their *Divine Essence*,
by encouraging them to become the failed part of you.

The *collective soul* is like a seed of grain,
it must be properly nourished
to preserve humanity *as a whole*.

Spirituality is my Reality, to cut the cord of sorcery illusions,
and to stay connected to the natural Essence
of the Divine Universe.

Expressions of the *Soul*, heals the *Soul*,
while resonating the frequency of *Love*. .

"You Made Me This Way..."
A bi-*Product* of my environment.
What did you expect for me to do with all of this
"Artificial Intelligence," ... Become artificial?!

Watch out... I'm operating at *Full Throttle*...
Blast Off!!

I'm not *troubled*... I'm simply *gifted*!

I don't compete. I conquer!!
Do you care for a challenge?!

No Worries!... No Stress!...
Each day, I will *thrive*, while doing my *Very Best!*

Being Great, is BEING GREAT!!...
What else is there to say!?

The *immoral creed* of humanity is *Greed*—
Rewards for misdeeds, brought against humanity as a whole.

When asked, what is my purpose in life, I respond,
"To be of <u>higher service</u> to Humanity." Which has become my
everyday therapy— *Writing inspirational poetry.*

You are a *Child of the Divine Universe.*
You are the *Collective Spirit of All beings.*
You are the *Power of Healing.*
You are *LOVE.*

Healing for Joy!… Is my *mantra.*
Today is the first day of more joyous days to come.

Today I put both feet forward, to become whole!

As the *Sun* shines *Love and Compassion* into my heart,
I shall never part from my duty and service
to help heal the *Soul of Humanity.*

Poetry, is my Therapy...

www.ingramcontent.com/pod-product-compliance
Lightning Source LLC
Chambersburg PA
CBHW070549160426
43199CB00014B/2428